# NOIR AFLOAT

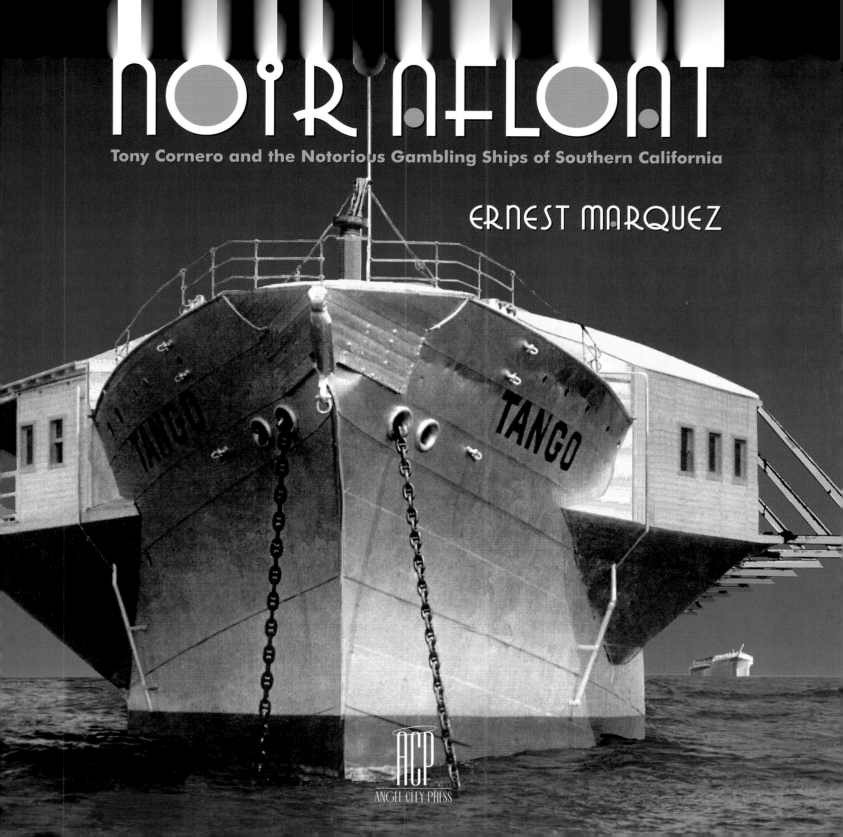

# NOIR AFLOAT

Tony Cornero and the Notorious Gambling Ships of Southern California

ERNEST MARQUEZ

ACP

ANGEL CITY PRESS

*Noir Afloat: Tony Cornero and the Notorious Gambling Ships of Southern California*
By Ernest Marquez
Copyright © 2011 by Ernest Marquez

Design by Amy Inouye, www.futurestudio.com
10 9 8 7 6 5 4 3 2 1

ISBN-13 978-1-883318-66-6

Library of Congress Cataloging-in-Publication Data

Marquez, Ernest, 1924-
 Noir afloat : Tony Cornero and the notorious gambling ships of Southern California / by Ernest Marquez.
   p. cm.
 Includes bibliographical references.
 ISBN 978-1-883318-66-6 (hbk. : alk. paper)
 1. Cornero, Tony (Anthony Stralla), 1900- 2. Gambling—California, Southern—History—20th century.
 3. Casinos—California, Southern—History—20th century. I. Title.
 HV6721.C2M37 2010
 795.09164'32—dc22
                        2010030701

ANGEL CITY PRESS
2118 Wilshire Blvd. #880
Santa Monica, California 90403
310.395.9982
www.angelcitypress.com

# CONTENTS

# Preface

From 1920 to 1933, the Volstead Act, or Prohibition, was in effect throughout the United States. Transportation, sale, and production of liquor was banned by the Eighteenth Amendment to the United States Constitution. Despite the law, enterprising bootleggers and rumrunners saw to it that Southern Californians who wanted liquor could have it—for a price. There were speakeasies in Los Angeles where you could buy a drink if you knew the password. Rumrunners smuggled liquor into California from Canada and became millionaires.

In 1929 the stock market crashed, leading to the Great Depression. Los Angeles was no different than anyplace else. Jobs were scarce, and many people stood in soup lines for a meal. Still, regardless of the difficulty almost everybody faced in maintaining a decent lifestyle, there were those who seemed to have enough money to squander it away by gambling.

Some public officials, who had promised to abide by the words in their oaths and by the rules and regulations of their office, reneged on that pledge. A few accepted bribes to do the bidding of lawbreakers, or to look the other way when unlawful activity took place. Even some police departments were corrupt. Cynics claimed it was difficult to distinguish between the criminals and the police. Los Angeles was like any other big city, where crime and corruption in all its forms were part of the everyday problems confronting honest officials and law-abiding citizens.

During this period, gambling operators seized the opportunity to create a new industry along the California coast: gambling ships. Gambling ship operators had no compassion for the downtrodden; they saw their patrons only as a source of income. If an individual was foolish enough to think he was going to win, he was ripe for the professional to empty his pockets, sending him home depressed and broke. The job of the operators was not to feel sorry for those they fleeced—it was their job to make gamblers feel as if they had a chance of winning even though the odds were against it.

Casino-type or percentage gambling was against the law within California's borders, but not on the open sea beyond the three-mile limit. The genius of the gambling ship operators was to anchor their casinos at sea just beyond the territorial limit and shuttle customers to them in water taxis. They advertised in the newspapers; they offered free passes, free dinners, free drinks, and free rides to lure customers to visit these unusual floating casinos. Who could turn that down? The public embraced the gambling ships as an entertaining distraction from the stresses of everyday life. People came by the thousands to lose their money.

Local, state, and federal authorities were at a loss to figure out how to shutter the gambling ships. City and state laws applied only within the state's borders, so the gambling ships were seemingly beyond their reach. From 1927 to 1939, a succession of ships avoided the law, and prospered. But in 1939, along came California's crusading attorney general Earl Warren. He brought the gambling ship era to its end, creating a story more fascinating than any Raymond Chander classic.

# PART I
# TONY CORNERO STRALLA

Known as the "King of the Rumrunners" and "Admiral of the Gambling Ship Fleet," Tony Cornero Stralla established that he had to be in charge of everything he touched.

*Opposite:* Cornero and his gang brought contraband from Vancouver and unloaded it at various locations along the Southern California coast. This map and images, printed in the *American Weekly Magazine* published by Hearst Newspapers, were part of a weekly exposé of the rumrunning business on the West Coast.

FRANK CORNERO.

TONY CORNERO.

WALTER SOUTH.

MELVIN SCHOUWEILER.

LOADING AT VANCOUVER.

SHIP'S PAPERS "FIXED" AT FOREIGN PORT.

LARGE BOATS BRING WHISKY SOUTH.

MACHINE GUNS USED TO KEEP OFF HIJACKERS.

POWER BOATS MEET RUM SHIPS AT SEA.

SKIFFS TAKE LIQUOR THROUGH SURF.

RUM BOATS LIE 50 TO 60 MILES OFF SHORE.

VANCOUVER

SAN FRANCISCO

SANTA BARBARA
OXNARD
LOS ANGELES
LONG BEACH
SEAL BEACH
DEL MAR
LAGUNA
OCEANSIDE
SAN DIEGO
SANTA CRUZ
CATALINA
SAN CLEMENTE

# Corruption in the City of Angels

Los Angeles in the 1920s and 1930s was promoted as a veritable earthly paradise, a blessed land of sunshine, and the healthiest possible place to live. It was proclaimed the nation's fastest-growing city, where land was cheap, and opportunities to get rich were unlimited.

What the promoters didn't mention was the seamy side of Los Angeles. A number of the city's highest elected officials were incompetent at best and dishonest at worst, and career civil servants openly accepted bribes. The Los Angeles Police Department was not only ineffectual, but corrupt. Critics claimed the police were no better than the city's criminals, and that it was often difficult to distinguish between the two.

In 1921, George Cryer became mayor, promising to combat crime and reform the police department. By the time he left office in 1929, Cryer had appointed no fewer than five different chiefs of police. Their collective previous experience totaled close to zero. Each in turn attempted one or another type of departmental reorganization; none succeeded. (Following Cryer, Mayors John C. Porter and Frank L. Shaw pledged to correct the sorry state of municipal affairs, but proved reluctant or unable to implement reform. Not until in 1938, when Fletcher Bowron was elected, would any real reform occur.)

Major crime ran rife in the 1920s Los Angeles, and an underworld mob known as the Big Five or the Spring Street Gang was responsible for most of it. The mob's leader, Charles Crawford, who owned both the Maple Bar on Fifth Street and a real estate office on Sunset Boulevard, boasted openly of having direct access— by way of a private telephone line—to "all the right places" in City Hall.

Crawford's mob worked as a team, but its members avoided any appearance of being linked. His mob included Albert Marco (a.k.a. Marco Albori), who controlled prostitution in the city; the brothers Joe and Bob Gans, who manufactured slot machines; Captain Guy McAfee, who was in charge of the Los Angeles Police Department's vice squad (known as the "Purity Squad") and ran a number of gambling houses on the side; Milton B. "Farmer" Page, who operated a bookie joint in his office on Spring Street; Tutor Scherer, a promoter and gambler who ran casinos as far away as Palm Springs; Chuck Addison, who was deeply involved in gambling; and Ezekiel "Zeke" Caress, a millionaire gambler, handicapper, and betting commissioner affiliated with the Agua Caliente racetrack in Tijuana.

**Opposite: Dedication ceremonies for the impressive new Los Angeles City Hall, built during the administration of Mayor George Cryer, were held May 6, 1928.**

S.S.REX

NOIR AFLOAT

Corruption in the City of Angels

The rackets in Los Angeles were ruled by Jack Dragna, a ruthless Mafioso, who operated independently of Crawford's mob until he began to appreciate the extent of its gambling and bookmaking ventures and was determined to cut himself in on the take. When Guy McAfee got wind of this and scornfully asked, "Who the hell is Jack Dragna?" he found out in short order. Dragna's henchmen held up McAfee's bookie joints and roughed up his runners to the tune of thousands of dollars. Dragna was cut in. But more significantly, Mafia-style violence and murder entered the Los Angeles gaming community.

Separate from the Spring Street Gang, bootleggers Marvin "Doc" Schouweiler and Tony Cornero Stralla both ran their own multimillion-dollar syndicates smuggling liquor into California during Prohibition.

In 1927, the $150,000,000 Julian Petroleum oil swindle, of dimensions to rival Teapot Dome, was uncovered in Los Angeles and riveted the attention of Angelenos for months to come. Grand jury indictments of perpetrators of this criminal fraud were handed down in July of 1927, but the trial was postponed until the end of January 1928. Instead of prosecuting the case himself, District Attorney Asa Keyes put his protégé and former secretary, only recently accepted by the California Bar and almost completely inexperienced in trial work, in charge of it. In May, when the jury finally had been selected and the trial was under way at last, Keyes suddenly announced that he planned to retire in six months. At one point during the trial proceedings, he asked the judge to dismiss charges against three of the defendants on grounds there was no evidence to prove them guilty.

# THE GOOD GUYS

**District Attorney Buron Fitts**

**Sheriff Captain George Contreras**

**Sheriff Eugene Biscailuz**

**Attorney General Earl Warren**

NOIR AFLOAT

Keyes, who had been in the courtroom only a few times during the trial, delivered the prosecution's closing statement. He astounded his audience, bewildered the jury, and directly contradicted the evidence put forward by his own deputy prosecutors by zeroing in on only one of the seven remaining defendants, declaring two others innocent, expressing doubts about the guilt of two others, and barely mentioning the remaining two. A day later, the baffled jurors found all seven men not guilty. Five months later came the revelation that Keyes had accepted bribes to guarantee acquittals. Refusing to resign, he insisted on finishing out the month left of his term. The *Los Angeles Times* of October 28, 1928, solemnly proclaimed that "the confidence of the public in its elected servants, the foundation point of the community, has been undermined to the danger point." Keyes was eventually brought to trial by Buron Fitts, his successor as district attorney, and sentenced to eight to ten years in San Quentin.

In 1929, John R. Porter, a former auto parts dealer, became mayor of Los Angeles. In his effort to re-form the police department, he demoted Chief of Police James Edgar Davis and appointed Davis's subordinate, Dick Steckel, to the post. Soon, Steckel himself became a figure in a major crime that decisively ended the ca-reer of mob leader Charles Crawford.

On May 21, 1931, Crawford and Herbert Spencer, editor of a reform-minded magazine, *The Critic of Critics*, were gunned down in Crawford's real estate office, in a double murder rendered more sensational when

# THE BAD GUYS

Asa Keyes steps aboard a train bound for San Quentin, accom-panied by Deputy Sheriff Frank Cochran.

Guy McAfee

Albert Marco

*Jack Dragna (ca. 1946).*

Jack Dragna

David Clark, a former deputy district attorney and a candidate for a judgeship, confessed to the killings. Taken into custody, Clark stated that Crawford and Spencer had proposed that he set up Chief Steckel for blackmail by sending him to a house in Santa Monica where he could then be "discovered" consorting with prostitutes. Clark claimed that when he turned down this proposition, Crawford became irate and reached for his gun, whereupon, in self-defense, Clark pulled his own gun and shot both men.

Indicted and tried for murder, Clark experienced a mistrial before his next trial produced a verdict of not guilty. Clark walked out of court a free man.

Los Angeles's next mayor, Frank L. Shaw, elected in 1933, pledged to deal effectively with the new and severe social and economic problems the city was experiencing as a result of the Great Depression and the inherited issue of internal corruption, particularly in the Police Department. Partway into his first term, however, he found himself the object of a wave of public detraction spearheaded by the Reverend Robert P. "Bob" Shuler, a well-known and highly articulate Methodist minister. Claiming that under Mayor Shaw "there is more vice, more crime, more debauchery, more graft in this city than there ever was before in its history," Reverend Shuler's denunciatory sermons and radio broadcasts astounded and aroused his listeners. His relentless anti-crime, anti-mayor, and anti-lawyer crusade earned him the sobriquet of "Fighting Bob."

Shaw spent much of his time defending himself against Fighting Bob and his adherents. He made

## THE MAYORS

**Mayor George Cryer**
**Served 1921-29**

**Mayor John R. Porter**
**Served 1929-33**

**Mayor Frank L. Shaw**
**Served 1933-38**

**Mayor Fletcher Bowron**
**Served 1938-53**

The California Brick was a block of compressed grapes that sold for two dollars. Its directions also cautioned readers: "Just place in a gallon of water for about six weeks to get a nice grape punch. Better drink it then, because if left longer it will ferment and will turn into wine."

little or no progress in the direction of reform and, for the most part, the public seemed disinclined to care. Managing to stay fed, clothed, and sheltered during a depression was too heavy a burden to allow time or energy for becoming active in civic reform. Before Shaw finished his term as mayor he was recalled and kicked out of office.

The passage of the Volstead Act in 1920 had ushered in an era unlike any the nation had ever experienced. Prohibition generated a change in people's attitudes toward ethical and moral absolutes, as well as a shift in the economy.

Products soon appeared that allowed everyone to make their own hooch. In California, grape growers produced the "California Brick," a block of compressed grapes and a legal item, which sold for two dollars. From it, the buyer could supposedly derive a tasty grape punch. Helpful instructions printed on each package warned against dissolving the brick in a gallon of water, adding sugar, shaking daily, and decanting after three weeks—clearly a recipe for homemade wine.

To a limited extent, California wineries were able to continue production by making wine for religious or medicinal purposes. The latter category included "wine tonics" or "wine elixirs," purported to be beneficial to health. Enterprises called "pharmacal laboratories" popped up in Los Angeles, selling such concoctions as Pep-Tol and Elix-All, which were nothing more than port or sherry wine fortified with twenty to twenty-two percent alcohol. These were ways to get around the law, but bootleggers and rumrunners depended on the fact that there was no way Americans would give up their freedom to drink, and they made illegal liquor available to anyone with the means to pay.

Ultimately, the proliferation of speakeasies and gambling casinos in backrooms of nightclubs in Los Angeles proper and all across Los Angeles County, with little or no interference from the police, became more than the average law-abiding citizen was willing to put up with. Reformers began pressuring the authorities to close such gambling establishments, and to put a stop to the crimes associated with them. The only result of their efforts was a series of token raids that looked impressive but never put the targeted speakeasy or casino permanently out of business.

Casino-type gambling at this time was illegal in California. Nevertheless, a group of innovative gambling operators openly and flagrantly plied their trade just slightly out of reach of the law, by locating casinos on vessels anchored in Pacific waters, slightly more than three miles from the shore. Even if a coastal town or city in Southern California had ordinances prohibiting gambling, its jurisdiction extended only to its shoreline. The same was the case for county authority jurisdiction. These gambling ships caused consternation among Southern California reformers and wrought havoc among infuriated city, county, state, and federal law enforcement agencies. Furthermore, law enforcement agencies had to confront a perplexing question: who had jurisdiction over these offshore casinos?

Far from being under cover, these pleasure palaces were visible from the shore by day and by night. Using newspaper and radio advertising, their operators broadcast their presence and attractions over the entire Southland. The gambling ship operators mailed and handed out thousands of invitations to the public, promising free shore-to-ship-to-ship transportation, free dinner on board, and diversified entertainment. Despite the deliberately

Even the image of a *padre* was summoned to bless this "elixir." Supposedly for medicinal use, California Padres Wine Elixir was sherry fortified with twenty-two percent alcohol. The truck is parked at the factory at Alameda and Macy Streets in Los Angeles.

innocuous wording of this publicity, the fact that the ships offered gambling games of every sort rapidly became the talk of the town. Civil authorities faced a jurisdictional problem in determining how to eliminate this ostensibly illegal industry.

State laws prohibited gambling casinos and percentage gambling within California's borders, but while its inland borders were well-defined, its ocean border at that time became the subject of contention because it did not follow the natural curvature of the shoreline, but lay three miles out to sea along an imaginary line known as the three-mile limit. There was an exception to this where a bay existed, in which case the three-mile limit lay three miles beyond an imaginary straight line connecting the bay's two headlands. The exact position of the three-mile limit in areas such as Santa Monica Bay, San Pedro Bay, and the Santa Barbara Channel became a heated debate between the gambling ship operators and local, state, and federal authorities, and, consequently, a matter for the courts to decide.

**A delivery vehicle disguised as a lumber truck featured removable panels that hid boxes of liquor so the contraband could be transported undetected through city streets.**

The waters from three to twelve miles offshore were under federal control. At that time, the federal government had no laws against gambling on land or sea. Beyond twelve miles from shore, the Pacific became part of international waters, where ships were subject only to the international laws of the sea. Taking advantage of the convenient absence of federal anti-gambling legislation, casino operators positioned their vessels inside federal waters and hired water taxis to ferry their patrons to them—to the utter frustration of local and state authorities.

A dozen different gambling ships operated from 1927 to 1939, each with its own owners or partners and backers. For the most part, these operators strived to remain anonymous to avoid the law. A flamboyant and outspoken man named Tony Cornero Stralla was the big exception. He was his own public relations agent and he made every effort to get his name in the paper. And he was determined to be known as the Admiral of the Gambling Ship Fleet.

# King of the Rumrunners

Anthony Cornero Stralla was born on August 19, 1900, on a farm in Italy's Piedmont District at the foot of the Alps. In 1904, his parents, Luigi and Maddalena Pirra Cornero, together with their sons, six-year-old Francis and four-year-old Anthony, immigrated to the United States. The little family settled in Los Gatos, California, a community of farms and vineyards south of San Francisco, already largely peopled by their countrymen. Barely a year later, Luigi Cornero was killed in an accident, and the widowed Maddalena subsequently married another immigrant, Giacomo Stralla. Tony and Frank, as they were known by that time, assumed their stepfather's surname, and when Giacomo was naturalized in 1914 they, too, acquired American citizenship. As time went on, they would also acquire a half-brother, Louis Stralla, and two half-sisters, Katherine and Madeline Stralla.

Throughout his life, Tony remained close to the family and devoted to his mother. He also retained a romantic pride in his origins, often expounding on the subject. "The Piedmont," he would declaim, "is not the part of Italy that breeds guitar players, opera singers, or the lower brackets of racketeers. If I do say so myself, the Piedmontese are a tough and hardy race of men, who till the soil and live to be ninety and up!" Tony, too, was tough and hardy, and in him the Piedmont had bred a racketeer of the highest order—one doomed for that very reason not to make it to ninety.

In 1915, when he was fifteen years old, Tony Cornero was convicted on three counts of robbery and sent to reform school. In 1918, he enlisted in the U.S. Naval Reserve, from which, after a summary court martial, he was discharged six months later for violation of orders, jumping ship, and remaining AWOL for various periods. After that, he drove a taxi in San Francisco until Prohibition became the law of the land in 1920.

Five years later, Tony Cornero, by then an ace at smuggling liquor into the United States, was a millionaire and the acknowledged king of Southern California rumrunners. He had accumulated a fleet of the largest and highest-powered speedboats money could buy, plenty of trucks and places to store contraband liquor, and a vast stable of rumrunners and agents. Almost all the liquor smuggled into California during Prohibition came from Canada, and the Cornero brothers (Frank Cornero was Tony's right-hand man) brought in only the best Scotch whiskey. "All the other stuff coming in," declared Tony, was "poisonous."

Operations as large as those of the Corneros were very decentralized enterprises. Cases of whiskey

*Opposite:* **Tony Cornero Stralla, seated in his chauffer-driven Cadillac, was a millionaire smuggler by the time he was twenty-five.**

NOIR AFLOAT

came south by the thousands in large vessels known as "mother ships," which dropped anchor at predetermined rendezvous locations in international waters, usually between thirty and fifty miles offshore. The Southern California coastline was far from ideal for smuggling. It lacked the hidden inlets and rocky apertures of the northern Pacific and Atlantic coasts. As a result, the process demanded darkness, silence, and maximum speed, and the rumrunners had to carefully make do with relatively unconcealed landing sites. The high-powered speedboats would race out to a mother ship, load the contraband, and speed back toward land, cutting their engines just clear of the surf line. At that point, the lucrative cargo would be shifted into dories, rowed to shore, and loaded into waiting trucks. The loaded trucks, with armed guards hanging on, ready to protect the haul from hijackers, transported the contraband to one or another "safe" location for temporary storage.

Tony's booze was expensive, but it wasn't all profit. With every shipment he had to pay off dozens of people: colluding agents within the Canadian exporting company and at the mother ship's stated Mexican or Central American destination to supply with false papers; the ship's captain and crew; the speedboat, dory, and truck crews; the armed guards; the owners of the storage locations and any nearby residents; and various local officials. All this expense, plus a hefty profit for Tony, meant that a bottle of Cornero's liquor could go for sixty-five dollars or more.

There was no secret about the identity of the big smugglers. Law enforcement authorities (and a good percentage of the public) knew well who they were. But they were frustrated by the fact that under the law they could arrest a ringleader only by catching him red-handed in possession of contraband within U.S. jurisdiction.

At twenty-five years of age, Tony Cornero was riding high. His business cards indicated he was an "importer" and "broker." He resided in a Beverly Hills mansion he had purchased for his mother. His public persona was that of a prosperous and friendly young businessman who mingled freely with both society figures and gambling racketeers, gladly spoke to the press, and wanted the world to know that he was engaged in saving citizens from poisoning themselves with "rotgut" liquor.

In the spring of 1926, Cornero traveled to British Columbia to arrange for a gigantic shipment of four thousand burlap bags (48,000 bottles) of good Scotch to be shipped from Vancouver to Los Angeles. The consignment was to be loaded early in June aboard a mother ship of Panamanian registry, the *Chasina*, which would sail south for about six weeks, reaching a rendezvous point some 150 miles off the Southern California coast at a location of quiet sea known as Tanner's Bank. It would take more speedboats than Cornero had to bring that much liquor ashore at one time, so he temporarily increased his fleet.

Amex Oil Company owned an elegant, eighty-four-foot, diesel-powered yacht named the *Donosari*. She was usually anchored at Wilmington, but mooring space was reserved for her at Long Beach as well. Unbeknownst to her owners—but not to Tony—the *Donosari* had already taken part in a few rumrunning expeditions. He now contacted the two men in charge of operating her, Gordon Grimstad and James Cunliffe, and arranged a deal.

Early on the morning of July 20, 1926, the *Donosari,* with Captain Grimstad at the helm and Cornero and one or two of his henchmen aboard, left her Wilmington berth and headed out to sea to meet the waiting

*Chasina*. Heavy waves slowed them down, and in the vicinity of Tanner's Bank, the sea was so rough and unruly that the *Chasina's* captain, H. H. Robinson, deemed it too dangerous for the big yacht to tie up alongside.

The only option was to drop anchor nearby and use the *Donosari's* dory to transfer the contraband cargo. Grim-faced and already frustrated at the loss of time, Cornero and his men began rowing back and forth, unloading the whiskey several bags at a time. They worked all through the night and into the next day, when an alarmed Captain Grimstad, afraid the yacht would be swamped, called a halt. Every available inch of space on the *Donosari* was filled with burlap bags, more than eight hundred in all. She was so weighed down that seawater was coming up through the sink outlets in her galley and head.

Late in the afternoon of July 22, the overloaded yacht began her wallowing journey back to land. A worried Cornero knew the men and equipment scheduled to meet her would no longer be waiting at shore point, and he ordered Grimstad to steer for Long Beach. Around 3 A.M. on July 23, the *Donosari* tied up to a piling in a deserted part of Long Beach Harbor. Ordering Grimstad to go home and keep his mouth shut, Cornero and his sidekicks took off to make new arrangements for completing what had become an extremely high-risk operation.

Cornero would have been more worried had he known that, even as the yacht was on her way to the *Chasina*, the president of Amex Oil, J.F. White, had issued orders for her to move from Wilmington to Long Beach. When the *Donosari* did not show up in a reasonable amount of time, he had told the police that he suspected she was engaged in illegal activity.

The *Donosari* lay unmolested until late that afternoon, when White decided to search for her himself and found her in the infrequently used Harbor Channel 3, looking considerably the worse for wear. With a surprising lack of caution, given the possibilities, he climbed aboard at once. Her interior was locked, but by peering through the windows of her salon, he could see bags piled to the ceiling. Guessing their contents, he debarked and went straight to police headquarters. A tug was sent out to tow her in, and by early evening she was properly moored at a municipal dock. Long Beach police broke open her hatches and realized instantly they would need more than their own vehicles to carry the sacks to proper storage. They called the fire department for help, and then set to work unloading the bags. The biggest available fire truck was pressed into service, along with police cars and policemen's private autos. The fire truck made no fewer than ten round trips to City Hall, where the bags were stowed on the upper floors. By midnight, the job was only half finished—in all, it took ten hours to confiscate the 806 loaded burlap bags.

The police noticed a man loitering in his car at one end of the dock, gazing fixedly at the unloading scene, sensed he might be in some way connected with the crime, and took him in for questioning. He identified himself as Louis Donalds, readily gave them a San Pedro address, answered their queries in a friendly and relaxed fashion, but gave them no reason to believe he had anything to do with the yacht or its contents, so they released him. The man was Tony Cornero.

Shortly thereafter, federal agents arrived. The identity of the *Donosari's* captain was ascertained, along with his nearby address. Police stationed themselves quietly outside his apartment, and when Grimstad emerged two days later, arrested him and took him to the city jail for questioning by the Feds. Grimstad told a long and involved story, claiming to have been victimized and forced by Cornero to sail the yacht to the mother ship. The only aspect of his tale the agents found credible was the mention of Tony Cornero, but that was sufficient grounds for arrest. When a mug shot of Tony was produced and Grimstad identified the likeness, the Long Beach police officers who had let "Louis Donalds" go were mortified. They led the ensuing search for the king of Southern California rumrunners, but by that time Cornero was long gone.

As officers went over the *Donosari* one more time, the total number of sacks confiscated rose to 817 (9,804 bottles)—an estimated sixty thousand dollars worth of liquor. What was not yet known was that Cornero's men, led by his brother Frank, had successfully smuggled 3,129 sacks from the *Chasina* to Sunset Beach, a few miles to the south.

When Cornero heard the news that the captain of the *Donosari* had been arrested and was talking to the police, Tony correctly reckoned that officers would be looking for him. A day or so later—if not sooner—Tony Cornero met his brother Frank at the eastern end of Olvera Street in downtown Los Angeles. Frank handed him a suitcase containing $150,000 in cash, and Tony continued across the street to Union Station, where he boarded a train for Seattle. Federal agents, alert to just such an escape attempt, were already watching all departure gates. Instead of identifying themselves and arresting Cornero, however, they followed him on board. Their theory was that he was actually heading for Vancouver, and would unknowingly lead them to even bigger game, since Canadian Exporters, Ltd. had become a major headache for Prohibition administrators all over the United States. Spotting is a two-way activity, however, and a racketeer can recognize a cop almost instinctively. Tony had indeed intended to go on from Seattle to Vancouver, but by the time the train was under way, he had devised an alternative route and settled back to enjoy the ride.

A good many hours later, as they neared the town of Redding in Northern California, Tony entered the men's room at the end of the car, quickly slipped out and onto the deck between the cars, and leaped off the train. Landing safely wide of the tracks, he picked himself up and raced toward a small airfield nearby. Finding a pilot and plane available, he flew to Portland, took a cab into that city, and reached the railroad depot in time to re-board the same train at its Portland stop. Cornero assumed the Feds had leaped off the train in pursuit and was surprised to see they were still aboard, sitting near his compartment. Retreating to another car before they caught sight of him, he bribed a porter to bring him his suitcase just as the train began pulling into Seattle. Then, undaunted, and with luggage in hand, he jumped onto the loading platform while the train was still slowing to a stop, walked briskly through and out of the station, and melted into the crowded street scene a free man.

Nine months after Tony Cornero had left the country, the *Los Angeles Times* of May 22, 1927, carried the following item:

> Tony Cornero, under federal indictment in Los Angeles, has left Canada and is on his way to his old home in Italy, according to word which reached federal authorities here yesterday.
>
> Cornero, sought since last August for smuggling in connection with the exposé of the

$10 million Consolidated Exporters Ltd. [of Canada] recently jumped from a speeding train near Seattle and escaped government officers.

Information reaching federal authorities in Los Angeles yesterday was to the effect that Cornero had boarded a ship at Vancouver, B.C. for Italy. Several months ago, the same report was received in Los Angeles, but the information reaching here yesterday was said to be authoritative.

In Hamburg, using the name Anthony Cornero Stralla, and identifying himself as representing Southern Freighters, Ltd., a Canadian company, which he had founded himself, he chartered a large German vessel, the *Przemsyl*, from her owner, Joseph Lassalle. The *Przemsyl* was then loaded with one hundred thousand gallons of alcohol (in ten-gallon cans), 419 barrels of whiskey, three barrels of sherry, two cases of essence of gin, and five cases of machinery (the makings of a still). The cargo was declared on the ship's manifest as destined for Vancouver, and she set sail on August 28, 1927. The manifest was false. The Captain's orders were actually to cross the Atlantic, go through the Panama Canal, turn north, and proceed up the Pacific coast to a rendezvous point about forty miles off San Diego.

The *Przemsyl*'s captain and first mate, however, decided to try a double cross. They sailed the vessel as far as Colon, at the eastern end of the Panama Canal, but then took her north to the port of New Orleans, planning to turn her cargo over as contraband to U.S. Customs there and to collect the sizable bounty offered for such a commendable act. By the time the customs office in New Orleans contacted "Mr. Stralla" to inform him the ship had been seized, the *Przemsyl* had been completely unloaded. Overnight, Frank Cornero and a bevy of lawyers appeared in New Orleans, charging barratry and insisting that the stated destination on the manifest was valid. Eventually, they won the day. The ship was reloaded, a new captain hired, and the conspirators turned over to the German embassy to be deported.

Not until late April of the following year (1928) did the *Przemsyl* head back to Colon, pass through the canal to Balboa, and start up the west coast of the United States.

Meanwhile, Tony Cornero, was holed up in Ensenada, Mexico. When the laden *Przemsyl* finally dropped anchor off San Diego in July 1928, he was waiting nearby aboard the steamer *L'Aquila*. One after another, rum-running speedboats arrived alongside the German vessel, and she began unloading cargo into them. Later, Tony sent the *Przemsyl* north to engage in similar activity in international waters off San Pedro, then further north near Santa Barbara. It was September before she returned to the San Diego location. Shortly thereafter, Cornero and speedboat driver George Garvin (whose water taxis would later carry crowds to and from Gambling Ship Row) were taking a last load off her when they sighted a Coast Guard cutter. The speedboat shot off under full power, and although the cutter gave chase, it was a hopeless pursuit. The Coast Guard gave up; the cutter returned to the *Przemsyl*, circled her a few times, and departed the area.

Ten years of dodging the law eroded Cornero's sense of freedom and power. He decided to face the consequences of the *Donosari* debacle. Accordingly, one bright fall morning, Anthony Cornero Stralla walked calmly into the Special Intelligence Unit of the Internal Revenue Service in Los Angeles. Deputy U.S. Marshal Vincent Mangarina was pleasantly surprised, but not unprepared. The king of the rumrunners was politely explaining his hope of engaging in a legitimate business, and his desire to clear up the charges pending against him, when Mangarina opened his desk drawer, pulled out the warrant for Tony's arrest he had been holding for almost three years, and served it.

Arraigned in federal court, Tony pleaded guilty to all three counts of the indictment that had been filed against him: violation of the National Tariff Act, conspiracy to violate it, and violation of the National Prohibition Law. Under questioning, he stated that he had had five separate liquor mobs working for him, as well as two hundred men under his direct supervision. Asked why he smuggled liquor into the United States, he replied, "I did it to keep 120 million people from poisoning themselves." He was convicted, fined $4,500, and sentenced to two years on each count, sentences to run concurrently and begin after a ten-day stay granted him for the purpose of winding up his affairs. Tony took advantage of that brief respite to discuss with his brother Frank and the rest of the Cornero-Stralla family how best to invest the formidable fortune he had amassed as a bootlegger. Characteristically, he had calculated that he would be out of action for at least a year and a half, and he was already focusing on what would happen after that. Less than three weeks later, in custody of federal marshals, he left Los Angeles by train for McNeil Island Penitentiary in Washington.

On the day Cornero turned himself in, both Los Angeles and Long Beach newspapers published reports of his capitulation to the authorities. The news did not, however, make their front pages, although it ordinarily would have. The date was October 29, 1929—Black Tuesday—and the headlines were the same across the entire United States. It was the worst day of the stock market crash, the start of America's Great Depression, and the end of the Roaring Twenties.

Despite a sagging economy and an American spirit that was at an all-time low, Tony Cornero, sitting in that Washington prison, was certain that there was big money to be made in Nevada, where gambling was a way of life. From behind penitentiary bars, he would mastermind and pay for the construction of the most impressive and luxurious gambling resort ever built in the United States—a Las Vegas extravaganza that would open in the summer of 1931.

# Las Vegas

Founded in 1905, Las Vegas was a sleepy little railroad town, which owed its existence to being the sole train stop between Los Angeles and Salt Lake City. In 1928, however, the United States government and the netherworld of gambling were about to change its image forever. The Boulder Dam Project and Tony Cornero arrived there at the same time.

When Nevada entered the Union in 1869, gambling was part of its culture. Unlike California, which had banned gambling in 1851, less than a year after attaining statehood, Nevada allowed it until 1911. That year, a wave of reform persuaded the Nevada legislature to declare gambling illegal throughout the state, so existing gaming facilities simply went underground, giving birth to a new underworld. Over the next two decades, back-room gambling dens proliferated, especially in Reno and the northern areas of the state. As enforcement of the gambling statutes gradually waned, however, such establishments emerged from the shadows. When their increasing visibility gave rise to no public clamor, and as the Depression deepened, enlightened state legislators recognized the extent to which revenue from purchases of gambling licenses, together with related fees, would help replenish Nevada's rapidly dwindling public treasury. In March 1931, they legalized gambling. Owners and operators came forward without hesitation, eager to pay for gambling licenses.

Clark County issued one of the first gambling permits to Frank Cornero Stralla and to Tony and Frank's younger half-brother Louis Stralla, Tony being otherwise occupied at the time. The permit was for their gambling resort, already under construction, well outside the Las Vegas city limits on the main road to the Boulder Dam site. They planned to name it the Meadows Club, "the meadows" being the English translation for *las vegas*.

Frank and Louis had arrived in the city soon after their brother's incarceration to lay the groundwork for the new enterprise and oversee every aspect of it. But they needed first to familiarize themselves with how things worked in Las Vegas and in Clark County. Second, but no less important, they needed to make clear that the new venture would escalate the prosperity of the community in a number of spectacular ways. It would relieve unemployment and enrich the area's businessmen, since all materials and supplies involved would be purchased locally; it would increase the county's financial base through its payments of taxes and fees; and it would ultimately draw millions of visitors, who would also patronize other establishments.

The brothers were well received. The idea of a gambling salon in the grand style—and the income to be derived from it—greatly appealed to the local power structure. So much so, in fact, that Frank Cornero was offered a lucrative deal on the side. Since its beginnings in 1905, and primarily at the behest of the railroad, Las

The Cornero brothers' Meadows Club, located on Charleston Boulevard, halfway between Las Vegas and Boulder Dam, was the first elegant gambling casino in Las Vegas.
*Opposite:* Going to Vegas was a dressy event, and the glamour was apparent at the Meadows Club roulette table.

Vegas had restricted its "red light district" to a single downtown block. Its houses of prostitution and its speak-easies were limited to Block 16, where both operated with impunity. Influential politicians—who wanted Block 16 torn down—gave Frank Cornero exclusive rights to the prostitution trade and promised to overlook liquor being poured, both in exchange for Frank moving the girls into the new resort's existing hotel that was due to be completely renovated and doubled in size. Frank accepted without hesitation.

Frank and Louis also learned that the city had only recently received a nasty shock, felt perhaps most strongly by its real estate interests, but also badly bruising its boom town enthusiasm.

Las Vegans were eagerly anticipating that thousands of workers hired to build the huge new dam would become Las Vegas residents for the duration. But when the Secretary of the Interior Ray Lyman Wilbur came to

Las Vegas

27
S.S. REX

In 1932, Fremont Street in Las Vegas was bustling. The Boulder Club, at 118 Fremont Street, and the Northern Club, at 15 Fremont Street (shown in the photo below), were among the first casinos to receive licenses when gambling was legalized in 1931.

Boulder Dam was the largest construction project in America. The Cornero brothers anticipated that workers from this gigantic project would be new customers for the Meadows Club in Las Vegas.
*Below:* Boulder City was planned to house five thousand people in 250 one-room cottages, 260 two-room houses, 123 three-room houses and fourteen other buildings with three to five rooms each. Single men lived in eight two-story dormitories.

Las Vegas

**Boulder City had its own business district. Boulder City Country Store catered to the needs of the new town's residents.**

visit, what he had to tell them was not what they had expected. Federal plans were to build Boulder City closer to the dam site, complete with housing for the six thousand dam workers and their families:

> It is the intention of the government that the bootlegger or other lawbreakers shall not interfere with the well being of its workmen. . . Instead of a boisterous frontier town, it is hoped that here simple homes, gardens with fruit and flowers, schools, and playgrounds will make this a wholesome American community.

The message was not only disappointing, but also downright insulting. Secretary Wilbur was wined and dined as planned, but hardly in a festive atmosphere, and few regretted his abrupt return to the East.

Despite that bad news, Las Vegas was still facing a rosy future. Supplies for Boulder would be shipped through the city and also stored there. Moreover, the hiring center was located in Las Vegas, as well as the Boulder Dam Administration Center and later all federal offices in Southern Nevada. As the dam rose higher and higher, the number of tourists was expected to grow accordingly. When 42,000 applicants from all over the country arrived to fill a mere six thousand jobs, with a goodly number of those not hired remaining in the city, municipal financial resources buckled under the strain. But even that crisis was averted when the New Deal went into effect and Congress provided welfare funds for the homeless.

Frank and Louis didn't worry that Boulder City would inhibit their success; there was no indication the

NOIR AFLONT

dam workers would be chained to their wholesome backyards. They surmised that those who weren't bringing families with them would certainly be ripe for entertainment and would doubtless be ready to gamble. Nor were they discouraged when the Block 16 deal collapsed after a local election broke the link between city and county powers and voided their unwritten agreement. Frank decided the presence of a few lively ladies imported from Los Angeles would still do well, not amount to much risk, and eliminate the need to pay off the bosses. They would open as planned, in late spring.

Indeed, Las Vegas was having a love affair with the Cornero brothers. On April 28, 1931, the *Las Vegas Evening Review Journal* treated its readers to the following:

> Las Vegas will soon be able to boast of a pleasure resort that will make Agua Caliente look like a hillbilly water tank," Harley A. Harmon, district attorney of Clark County, proudly announced during a visit to the state Capital. "Reno had better look to its laurels as the Monte Carlo of America. A new resort, the Meadows, is being erected by Frank Cornero and Louis Stralla, Los Angeles capitalists . . . no expense is being spared in the venture. . . , and the elaborate landscaping and buildings will make the place one of the real beauty spots of the West.

**For the convenience of its elite clientele who would rather fly than drive, there was a small airfield near the Meadows Club.**

**The highfalutin interior and clientele of the Meadows Club intimidated the Boulder Dam workers, who preferred the smaller Sawdust Joints. Soon, even the matchbooks tried to promote the club as "not formal."**

The Meadows was clearly a modern rendition of a California mission, with its long shady portico extending almost the full length of its front, church-sized doors, and a high center façade, seemingly awaiting the installation of a cross, not the neon logo of an entertainment palace. A generous courtyard and gently playing fountain enhanced the paradox inside. Within its walls were neither pews nor statues, but instead a deep-carpeted casino, nightclub and a ballroom, all palatial and elegantly draped, decorated, and richly furnished. Behind the main building lay the twenty-five-room hotel, soon to be enlarged to one hundred rooms.

The grand opening on May 2, 1931 was a formal event attended by hundreds, including many Southern California celebrities and most of Nevada's professional and political power structure. Frank, Louis, and their mother did the honors, and every guest was made to feel important. In addition to the delights of the casino, there was music by the club's own band, the Meadow Larks, imported from Los Angeles, and a dazzling floor show produced for the occasion by a master of the trade, Jack Laughlin of New York and Hollywood. Although Prohibition was still in effect, gallons of the best champagne were consumed in the course of the gala evening. Years later, Nevada journalist and historian John Cahlan summed it up: "That was the opening that set the stage for all future resort hotel openings in Las Vegas."

Early in the morning of September 7, 1931, a fire of suspicious origin broke out in the kitchen area of the Meadows hotel. A truck from Las Vegas tore off to the scene of the conflagration, but stopped short at the city limits. The fire captain informed frantic emissaries from the Meadows that he had been ordered not to enter county territory to fight a fire. Meadows personnel did their best with garden hoses and portable extinguishers, but a considerable portion of the hotel burned to the ground.

Such arbitrary and outrageous default by the city's fire department created local furor, so city officials responded in the *Las Vegas Evening Review Journal* with the following explanation:

> The solution. . . does not lie in sending fire apparatus outside city limits. It is. . . the reverse . . . [i.e.,] the presentation of a petition to the City Board by a majority of the property owners in the outlying district that desire protection, requesting that the city limits be extended to include them. Those still wishing to remain outside the city for reasons of their own would be expected to provide their own fire protection in return for the benefits of operating beyond city borders.

The cat was out of the bag! City powers were well aware that Tony Cornero would not ask to be included within the city limits, because, as a convicted felon, he was not eligible for a city gambling license.

Trouble of a different nature lay ahead for the Meadows. Although it continued to be a center of social events for Las Vegas and Boulder City society, the thousands of patrons Tony had envisioned did not materialize. Many of the ordinary dam workers tried out the Meadows, but only a few returned regularly. They felt ill at ease in such a luxurious setting, rubbing elbows with ladies in fancy gowns and obviously well-moneyed men—particularly knowing their high-level supervisors might be among them. As a result, they took to driving right on past the resort and into Las Vegas proper, where they would not feel out of place in boots and jeans—and where numerous no-nonsense sawdust-on-the-floor gambling joints provided their kind of a good time.

Within a few years, the brothers agreed it was time to cut their losses. They sold the hotel and leased the casino, nightclub, and ballroom to three associates, one of whom was reputedly a power in the caterers' union. Louis Stralla returned to Northern California to run the family winery there. Frank stayed on, working for the new operators, but the Meadows steadily declined toward a sorry end, gradually becoming little more than a whorehouse. On November 4, 1935, it closed for good.

Frank Cornero explained it all with hindsight: "The Meadows was ten years before its time. Las Vegas wasn't ready for an elegant casino yet."

Tony Cornero remained convinced that the gambling trade remained his best route to fortune and success. Having heard about the success the gambling ships were having along the coast of California, he departed for Los Angeles.

# The *Tango*

W hen Tony Cornero Stralla was released from prison in 1930, he promised his parole officers he would become an honest businessman. Cornero fully intended to avoid breaking the law, but his unique morality saw nothing wrong with finding ways to skirt the law. Though gambling remained illegal in California, he witnessed the gambling ships survive both police raids and court trials. Tony Cornero saw his future.

The *Tango* was originally built in 1904 at Glasgow, Scotland, for German owners and given the name *Hans*. She was a four-masted steel ship and, for a time, the largest sailing vessel in the world. When World War I broke out, she was anchored along with eleven other German ships in the Mexican seaport of Santa Rosalia on the Baja California peninsula. Fearing the ships would be seized if they entered any other than a neutral port, their German owners ordered them to stay put until the cessation of hostilities.

After Germany was defeated, the Allies took over all German ships interned at Santa Rosalia. Subsequently, in accord with the Treaty of Versailles, they were turned over to the War Reparations Commission, which in 1920 awarded the *Hans* to Great Britain. Robert Dollar, of the Dollar Lumber Company in Northern California, who had already expressed an interest in the *Hans*, purchased her for his fleet for $27,000, and renamed her the *Mary Dollar*. By the time the *Mary Dollar* reached San Francisco, the shipping industry

**The freighter *Mount Baker* and the four-masted bark *Mary Dollar* laid up together at Oakland Creek in northern California to await an unknown future. Eventually, they both became gambling ships.**
***Opposite:** **Mary Dollar** was completely transformed into the **Tango**. She lost her beautiful image as an elegant sailing vessel and soon anchored off Long Beach, alongside three other vessels on Gambling Ship Row.*

NOIR AFLONT

WEST SEVENTH ST. WATER TAXI CO.
DIRECTIONS FROM LONG BEACH

WEST 7TH ST.        1315 W. 7TH. ST.
                                    SECOND WATER
                                    TAXI PARKING
                                    LOT

Second Water
Taxi Parking Lot    *Look* FOR SIGN
on 7th Street       **TANGO**
West of Pico

PICO TO W. 7. ST.

ANAHEIM TO PICO
**FREE PARKING**

Serial № 16397 A
THIS CARD ENTITLES the HOLDER TO
**TWO FREE CARDS**
IN OUR
"BIG $50.00 ADVERTISING GAME"
OF TANGO ANY MONDAY AT 10:00 p.m.
There are Absolutely No House Players at Any
Time in This Game.

35
"S.S. REX"

**The *Tango***

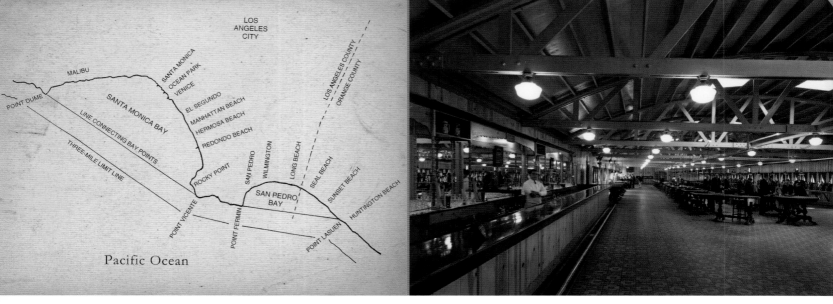

The three-mile limit was at the heart of every legal battle over the gambling ships' location. This map defines it.
*Above right:* The vast interior of the *Tango* has room for a huge array of gambling games.

had sunk into postwar depression. As it revived, older vessels were replaced by steamships built during the war, and the big steel four-master never sailed again. She was discarded on the mud flats of Oakland Creek, where she deteriorated for eleven years, her value steadily declining. On October 3, 1934, she was purchased for $3,500 by Captain Charles Watts, acting as agent for a gambling syndicate. A condition of the sale was that she be immediately renamed, so she could in no way be connected to the Dollar Steamship Lines. She was renamed the *Tango*. On New Year's Day of 1935 she began her next journey to San Pedro, towed by the steam schooner *Dan F. Hanlon*, which was also carrying a full load of lumber.

As soon as the two vessels cleared San Francisco Bay, trouble began: seventy-mile-per-hour winds broke the towline, leaving the *Mary Dollar* adrift and at the mercy of the storm. The captain of the *Dan F. Hanlon* found his heavily loaded ship almost impossible to maneuver; nor was her crew able to get a new hawser over to the older vessel. Given the severity of the gale, the steamer could only take care of herself, so she continued southward. Aboard the *Mary Dollar*, Captain Watts and his crew of nine managed to maneuver the craft for about forty miles to a safe spot south of Point Reyes, and dropped anchor to wait for help.

After sunrise a Coast Guard cutter found the four-master and radioed for a tug, then two more days passed before the Red Stack tug *Sea Monarch*, sent from Los Angeles, towed her to the Patten Blinn Lumber Company dock at Wilmington for conversion into a gambling ship. The procedure that ensued reflected the arrogant and brutal ethos of her new owners.

Workers cut away the schooner's 198-foot steel masts, tore out her superstructure, and widened her main deck by building platforms beyond the width of the hull on either side of it. Having thus destroyed her graceful profile, they erected the deck's new gambling casino—a wooden, barn-like structure 240 feet long

and fifty feet wide. By the time they finished, nothing hinted that she had once been a magnificent sailing ship. Finally, to stabilize her, they dumped five hundred tons of sand over the hardened copper slag still left in her hull from the years in Santa Rosalia. Thus defaced, the *Tango* ex-*Mary Dollar* ex-*Hans* was ready for her debut. Pulled by two tugs, she moved out past the three-mile limit and joined three other gambling ships, the *Monte Carlo*, the idle *Johanna Smith II*, and *Casino*, all anchored off Long Beach. In 1935, after leaving Las Vegas, Tony Cornero and his friend and financial backer James Lloyd each put up fifteen thousand dollars to join the syndicate that was about to launch the *Tango*, destined to be a gambling ship extraordinaire.

The syndicate included the ubiquitous Clarence Blazier, "Doc" Schouweiler, and Calvin Cluster, a gambler who owned a club at Lake Tahoe near the California-Nevada border. As a partner and for the sake of gaining the knowledge and experience he needed to run a floating casino of his own, Tony had to repress his ever-present need to be the boss.

The *Tango* was Tony Cornero's first venture into the floating casino trade. But he was no stranger to coastal waters, having come to know them well during his rumrunning days during Prohibition. Moreover, he was completely familiar with the intricacies of casino gambling, having learned at his own gambling den, the Meadows. He was now about to launch a career as the most famous and flamboyant Southern California gambling ship owner.

The *Tango* was state of the art. Her shipmaster and crew carried seamen's union papers. Their primary responsibility was to keep the ship seaworthy and in position. Crewmen might assist passengers from water taxi to deck but they had nothing to do with the gambling operations. The ship's operators took pains to accommodate the professional gamblers among their clientele. Whenever a film

**WORLD'S LARGEST PLEASURE SHIP**
**S. S. TANGO**
**MORE EXCITING THAN THE RACES**

**Odds Payable to Owners of Winning Chances**

| | |
|---|---|
| Any Number betted | 35 to one |
| Two Numbers betted with one coin | 17 " " |
| Three Numbers betted | 11 " " |
| Four Numbers betted (in a square) | 8 " " |
| Five Numbers (including 0 and 00) | 6 " " |
| Six Numbers (transverse line across) | 5 " " |
| Twelve Numbers (in a column) | 2 " " |
| First 12 (means 1 to 12) | 2 " " |
| Second 12 (means 13 to 24) | 2 " " |
| Third 12 (means 25 to 36) | 2 " " |
| Red (any red number) | 1 " " |
| Black (any black number) | 1 " " |
| High (19 to 36) | 1 " " |
| Low (1 to 18) | 1 " " |
| Odd (any odd number) | 1 " " |
| Even (any even number except 0 and 00) | 1 " " |

**Free instruction cards explained the rules for roulette.**

It's easy to get to the S. S. TANGO

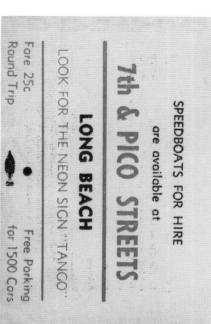

Fare 25c
Round Trip

Free Parking
for 1500 Cars

SPEEDBOATS FOR HIRE
are available at

7th & PICO STREETS

LONG BEACH

LOOK FOR THE NEON SIGN "TANGO"

Enjoy a picturesque speedboat ride thru the Battle Fleet to the S. S. Tango

star or other celebrity was playing in the casino, a crowd would invariably gather to watch, and the same thing would happen when a professional gambler was in action—an unwanted distraction at best. To afford such gamblers privacy, a special room was built below the main deck. Guards made sure only professional high rollers or other people cleared by the bosses ever entered this elite den.

While the *Tango*'s dining room observed the usual gambling ship custom of serving free turkey dinners to all customers, such luxuries as prime rib, steak, and lobster were also available, though not free. At seventy-five cents apiece, drinks were expensive for the time, but patrons could expect one free, their hosts counting on them to gamble away at least the cost of dinner and a drink, and usually much more.

By 1938, Tony Cornero and Clarence Blazier remained

**Cards were handed out on the street advertising the *Tango*.**
***Left:* Invitations that folded into a postcard-size mailer were available on the ship. Visitors could address the mailer and send it to a friend, an early example of creative marketing.**

NOIR AFLOAT

in charge of the *Tango*, with Blazier now general manager. Cornero, a strong-willed young man with definite ideas of his own, had little respect for the management style of the more experienced Blazier. Cornero openly challenged Blazier by suggesting that more money could be made if they lowered the odds on bets.

Blazier rejected Tony's suggestion. Possessed of a fiery temperament, and accustomed to his ideas being carried out without question, Cornero refused to back down.

Tony challenged Blazier, "Let's roll the dice. Winner take all. My share against your share."

Tony Cornero rolled. . . and lost. His interest in the *Tango* was reputed to be worth $97,000, but he left the ship without remorse. He delighted in recounting the incident, frequently explaining: "I've got to be the boss of everything I touch, so I'm sure things go right. Any other way, I'm not sure." Cornero told exaggerated stories about himself, and this may have been one of them. Nevertheless, Cornero severed his relations with the *Tango* syndicate and began a spectacular career as boss of his own gambling ship.

By the end of the 1930s, the public viewed the gambling ships on the horizon less as a wretched intruder and more as a shady but inevitable component of the coastal entertainment scene. That such vessels were known venues of crime and haunted by criminal types was obscured by the crowds of regular working folk frequently patronizing the ship. The worst of the Depression was over in Southern California. More and more middle-class workers had pulled out of financial desperation and were able to indulge in the occasional splurge. With twenty-five cents for a water taxi ride and armed with a ticket for a free dinner to celebrate an important occasion or impress out-of-town visitors, locals would fly over the waves to enjoy a sophisticated evening under the stars—and with the Hollywood stars—aboard a palatial floating casino.

The *Tango* anchored at sea just beyond the three-mile limit, held in place by four heavy anchors.
*Left:* The *Tango*'s Gold Award came out of a slot machine when the customer hit the jackpot, and could be exchanged for cash.

# Kenilworth/Star of Scotland/Rex

n old fishing barge lying at anchor off Santa Monica caught Tony Cornero's eye, and he persuaded James Lloyd to partner with him again and buy her. The vessel they purchased was the *Star of Scotland*, then rounding out a half century of service. Built in 1887 by John Reid and Company of Glasgow for the British Waverly Line and originally named the *Kenilworth*, she started life as a beautiful four-masted windjammer. She was steel-hulled, three hundred feet long, and boasted a striking figurehead of Mary Queen of Scots at her prow. The sight of her approaching San Francisco under full sail on her maiden voyage from Scotland would have thrilled any sailing-ship lover.

The *Kenilworth*'s shipping career nearly ended permanently on August 26, 1889. On that day, she was moored alongside two wooden vessels at McNear's Wharf at Port Costa in Carquinez Strait, northeast of San Francisco, waiting to be loaded with grain destined for England. A fire broke out in an adjacent warehouse. The flames spread to the sails of the two wooden vessels and, as wharf hands rushed to untie both ships, sparks flew into the *Kenilworth*'s rigging. Mooring lines were cast off, and all three ships, burning furiously, drifted out into the deep waters of the strait in one horrifying mass of flame. The two wooden vessels were completely destroyed, and only her steel hull saved the *Kenilworth*. She was so badly damaged by the conflagration, however, that her

The four-masted windjammer originally called *Kenilworth* was sold to the Alaska Packers Association in 1908 and became part of its salmon fishing fleet under the name *Star of Scotland*.
*Opposite:* Sold again in 1930, *Star of Scotland* became a fishing barge anchored off the shores of Santa Monica.

*Kenilworth/Star of Scotland/Rex*

41
S.S. REX

Fishermen loved the barge. With gunny sacks loaded with their catch, these fishermen are preparing to board a boat to take the fish back to land. The ship had a small galley and the menu read, "Bring your own fish in prepared for cooking, and our chef will be glad to cook and serve them with Potatoes, Bread and Butter, and Coffee"—all for forty cents per order.

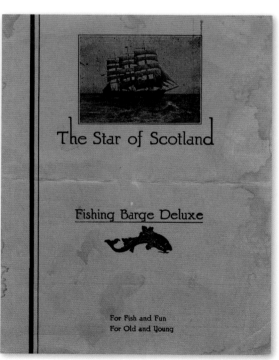

The Star of Scotland

Fishing Barge Deluxe

For Fish and Fun
For Old and Young

NOIR AFLOAT

In this photograph, fishermen work on the bow of the vessel, and the back of the head of the figurehead Mary Queen of Scots can be seen facing out to sea.

owners abandoned her to their insurance underwriters, who sold her "as is" to Arthur Sewall & Company of Bath, Maine. Her new owners had the *Kenilworth* brought back to seaworthy status at the Union Iron Works in San Francisco, and for the next eighteen years she plied the seas in the Cape Horn trade.

In 1908, the Alaska Packers Association bought the *Kenilworth*, renamed her *Star of Scotland*, and started her on eighteen more years of service, primarily consisting of annual voyages to the Bering Sea, from which she would return with her hold filled with canned salmon. They retired her from service in 1926, but her working years were still far from over. In 1929, Southern California business partners Charles Arnold, Lewis Lockhart, and A.O. Pearce purchased the *Star of Scotland* from Alaska Packers and had her towed to Santa Monica. In 1930, she opened there as a fishing barge, two miles straight out from the pier, still carrying her four tall masts, but without rigging and sails.

In her new role, the *Star of Scotland* became the delight of local fishermen. Platforms were attached to her sides, enabling fishermen to get closer to the water to fish with jackpoles. Moreover, fishermen could rent a stateroom on board and stay for the weekend. Galley cooks stood at the ready to clean and cook one's catch for forty cents, or serve up a plate of chili for twenty-five cents, or a hamburger for ten cents. Live bait was free. Fishing poles could be rented for a dollar a day. The *Star of Scotland* emulated the practice of other fishing

**After Cornero bought the *Star of Scotland*, she was placed in dry dock at the Los Angeles Shipbuilding Company at San Pedro, where she underwent her conversion to a gambling ship.**

barges in the area by providing a couple of nickel and dime slot machines on board as diversions. It was illegal, of course, but police seldom bothered to confiscate them. Thus, from 1930 to 1937, the big windjammer served as a source of pleasure for those who patronized her.

In Tony Cornero's imagination, however, the ship took on a far less aesthetic appearance. He saw her as the floating palace he was seeking, and was delighted to find that her owners were willing to sell their popular fishing barge for twenty-three thousand dollars. A sales agreement, calling for an initial payment of ten thousand dollars and the balance in five-hundred-dollar monthly installments, was signed and witnessed.

Cornero renamed his new ship the *Rex*, a Latin word defined as "the reigning king." It was also the name of what was then Italy's newest and largest ocean liner.

In dry dock at the Los Angeles Shipbuilding Company, workers dismantled and rebuilt the *Rex* for her new career. Her steel hull was cleaned of barnacles, seaweed, moss, and other sea life. The fishing platforms were removed from her sides. All four towering masts were cut down. The superstructure on her main deck

The *Star of Scotland* was completely changed from a beautiful sailing ship to a floating gambling casino called *Rex*. Her new name was completely visible when she was anchored off Santa Monica.

was cleared away, and a three-hundred-foot-long deckhouse—the future casino area—took its place. When the transformation was complete, not a single hint of her original beauty remained. Tony claimed the refurbishing had cost $350,000. He rated her gorgeous, and incorrectly embellished her name with the title "S.S."

In April of 1938, Cornero approached E.J. and Ray McGough, two brothers who jointly owned the Santa Monica Boat Service, which ran water taxis to and from vessels moored in Santa Monica Yacht Harbor. The Mc-Goughs held permits from the California State Railroad Commission allowing them to provide boat service to San Pedro and Catalina, and Cornero struck an amicable and profitable deal with them to ferry patrons to and from the *Rex*.

Aware that they would soon see a tremendous increase in ridership, the McGoughs sought and received city permission to renovate and reopen an old waiting room on the lower deck of the Santa Monica municipal pier, and to anchor a large float with gangplanks adjacent to it.

Tony created a new Nevada corporation, called Rex, Inc. Its officers of record were himself, A. Stralla, president; James Lloyd, vice-president; and Jean Stralla (Tony's wife), secretary. Ironically, he was determined to do everything right. He insisted that every *Rex* employee be an American citizen and, for good measure, took their fingerprints and sent them to the police.

On April 29, Cornero applied to the Santa Monica department of public works, which controlled the electrical system on the city's pier, for a permit to erect a large neon sign at the end of the structure. The department's head, Commissioner W.W. Milliken, promptly denied the request. Always looking for a loophole, Cornero asked if he could install the sign if he supplied its electricity from an outside source. The request was refused. Cornero subsequently had the sign redesigned and mounted on the old, privately owned Looff Pleasure Pier, which was connected to the municipal pier. The new sign consisted only of a giant "X," followed by a small arrow pointing to the adjacent taxi landing.

# The *Rex*

On May 1, 1938, a tug came chugging into Santa Monica Bay towing the *Rex*. The big vessel had no means of self-propulsion, since the only engines on board ran its electrical generators and a donkey engine that lifted her four anchors. At a point exactly three and one-half miles from the Santa Monica shoreline, the anchors were dropped—two at her bow and two at her stern—leaving the *Rex* firmly in place and in view of land.

Reporters from the local papers were quick to ride out to the S.S. *Rex*. Like any proud proprietor, Cornero provided an informative tour of his floating palace. First he showed the lower deck's five-hundred-seat bingo parlor and the stern's horse-race betting parlor. He then presented the *piece de resistance,* the grand casino on the upper deck, which extended the entire length of the vessel and featured eleven roulette tables running down its center. Around them were eight dice tables, blackjack and faro games, a Chinese lottery, and numerous other intriguing gambling devices. A long wall on one side of the casino was entirely taken up by a liquor bar, while the other was lined with 150 slot machines. Two dining rooms and a dance floor meant customers could dine, dance to a live orchestra, or watch a floor show.

The slots had been supplied by Bob Gans, known as the Slot Machine King of Los Angeles, who received a quarter of the profits from them. Tony made a point of saying that, except for the fact that patrons expected them, he would just as soon not have slot machines on the *Rex*. Asked why, he explained that each machine took fifteen cents out of every dollar bet, and with that margin, soon acquired all a player's money. He mentioned that he had some of them adjusted—if a player won nothing in the course of ten plays, his money was returned. The reporters were duly impressed, agreeing on the trip back to shore that Tony Cornero, despite his checkered past, certainly seemed a decent fellow.

Weeks earlier, when it was first reported that the *Rex* was coming to Santa Monica, anti-gambling ship sentiments again surfaced in the city. As days passed with no indication that authorities planned to intervene, the rumble of protest grew louder among local religious, financial, and social groups. A delegation of outraged dignitaries stormed the office of Santa Monica Mayor Edmond Gillette. They informed the mayor that his administration was failing to carry out its civic duty and demanded he get rid of the *Rex* without delay. Flustered by their intensity, Mayor Gillette assured them he intended to use any legal means at his disposal to banish the *Rex*.

Not everyone present was against the *Rex* for moral reasons. A group of yacht owners from Santa Monica and surrounding areas, whose craft were moored in the city harbor, argued that the city had built the harbor for pleasure boats, and that taxis moving in and out of it constituted a hazard and, worse, interfered with boat

NOW ANCHORED OFF
# SANTA MONICA
### BEYOND THE 3 MILE LIMIT
Only 10 minutes from Hollywood then a comfortable 12-minute boat ride to the REX. Continuous water taxi service TO and FROM ship, 25c round trip from Santa Monica Pier at foot of Colorado Street, Santa Monica. Look for the red "X" sign. Park on pier.
### WE NEVER CLOSE
DINE and DANCE to the Rhythm of the REX MARINERS. Cuisine by Henri — Cocktail Lounge — Popular Prices
RACING SERVICE DESCRIPTION from All Tracks Beginning at 9 a.m. Every Day. WE PAY TRACK ODDS, A▶ TRACKS

PLAY Bingo on the Rex

S.S. REX

WORLD'S LARGEST CASINO

*Cornero started a massive advertising campaign for his gambling ship. Thousands of cards promoting the ship were handed out on the street, and newspapers published his advertisements.*

and yacht races scheduled throughout the summer. They reminded the mayor that private craft moored in the harbor were also a source of revenue for the city.

Cornero, who for days had been promoting the *Rex* with a major publicity campaign, continued to advertise her upcoming opening on May 5. Southern California newspapers carried full-page ads illustrated by a drawing of a sleek three-stack ocean liner. Skywriters flew over Los Angeles County from one end to the other, leaving huge white Xs and the letters "R E X" behind them to slowly fade against the blue. Tony had instructed their pilots to maintain an altitude of at least three miles, in case state jurisdiction turned out to be three-dimensional. In urban areas of Los Angeles and the beach cities, a number of the chronically jobless found temporary employment passing out business cards with "S.S. *Rex*" on one side and, on the other, tickets for free water taxi rides and a free dinner on board.

Concerned that contracting for gambling promotions on California soil might be against the law, Tony made all his business arrangements on board the *Rex* and paid for them in cash on the spot. Compulsive in his need to personally manage any enterprise he was involved in, he did not hesitate to write his own advertising. Cornero wrote as freely and flamboyantly as he spoke. In an amazing departure from gambling-trade norms, he produced the following widely published declaration:

I, Tony Cornero Stralla, agent for the S.S. *REX*, anchored three miles off Santa Monica Pier, do hereby challenge any movie or radio star, sponsor or broadcasting station, newspaper, or any other person or persons to find on board the S.S. *REX* any illegally or crookedly operated games. If anyone, and I mean ANYONE, can find aboard the S.S. *REX* a falsely run game, then I will pay to that person or persons the sum of ONE HUNDRED THOUSAND DOLLARS ($100,000.00) cash on demand. The S.S. *REX* is run honestly and above board and is operated by courageous, open-minded, fearless American citizens.

(Signed) TONY CORNERO STRALLA,
Agent, S.S. *REX*

P.S. Furthermore, crooked gambling on the high seas is punishable by imprisonment in a Federal penitentiary by Federal Statutes and is strictly enforced. This statement concerns only the S.S. *REX* anchored off Santa Monica at the foot of the Santa Monica Pier and in no way affects what might happen on other boats. This statement is issued as an invitation to board the S.S. *REX* and inspect any game equipment at any time.

After making sure his employees read this ironclad guarantee, Cornero, one step ahead of them, warned that it was not his intention to ever pay out the money. He said, "Don't even think about having one of your friends come out to the ship and catch you cheating, because you'll be floating in the Pacific before you get any reward."

On May 5, 1938, the palatial floating casino opened for business and became an overnight success.

Although Cornero could be tough when necessary, he treated his ship's staff with gentlemanly respect and paid them generously. At the time, the salary of a general office worker averaged six to twelve dollars a week. Dealers on the *Rex* earned ten dollars a day plus tips. Pit bosses earned twenty-five dollars a shift.

**Cornero wanted everybody to know about his gambling ship. He sent up skywriters to emblazon REX for Southern Californians to see. He even told the pilots to fly higher than three miles in the sky, in case there was a three-mile limit there, too.**

Like all successful offshore gambling ships, the *Rex* drew customers from every walk of life. Hollywood types representing almost every facet of that industry frequented her tables. Professionals of every sort not only enjoyed an occasional visit, but found her especially useful when they had out-of-town guests to entertain. Blue-collar and white-collar workers came in droves. For tourists, the *Rex* was a must-see. Even unescorted ladies, courteously helped into and out of the water taxis and politely welcomed aboard, felt free and safe to enjoy a few hours in the casino. For the younger set, in couples or groups, an evening aboard her was the height of sophistication. Many found the spray-flecked rides over the waves and dancing to the music of the ship's orchestra, the Rex Mariners, to be the ingredients of an exciting and romantic evening.

Even people with no interest in gambling or no money to spare would visit the ship. Almost every night, a subset of the customers came just to claim their free meal. After partaking in their feast, they bypassed

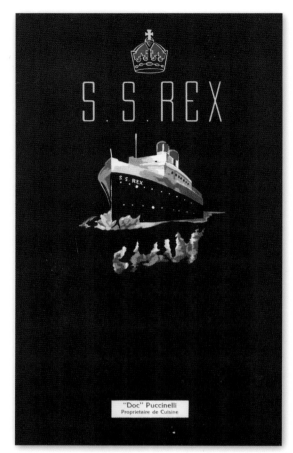

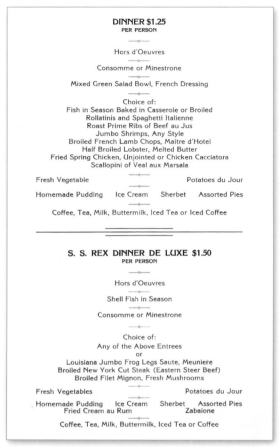

**DINNER $1.25**
PER PERSON

Hors d'Oeuvres

Consomme or Minestrone

Mixed Green Salad Bowl, French Dressing

Choice of:
Fish in Season Baked in Casserole or Broiled
Rollatinis and Spaghetti Italienne
Roast Prime Ribs of Beef au Jus
Jumbo Shrimps, Any Style
Broiled French Lamb Chops, Maitre d'Hotel
Half Broiled Lobster, Melted Butter
Fried Spring Chicken, Unjointed or Chicken Cacciatora
Scallopini of Veal aux Marsala

Fresh Vegetable                    Potatoes du Jour

Homemade Pudding   Ice Cream   Sherbet   Assorted Pies

Coffee, Tea, Milk, Buttermilk, Iced Tea or Iced Coffee

**S. S. REX DINNER DE LUXE $1.50**
PER PERSON

Hors d'Oeuvres

Shell Fish in Season

Consomme or Minestrone

Choice of:
Any of the Above Entrees
or
Louisiana Jumbo Frog Legs Saute, Meuniere
Broiled New York Cut Steak (Eastern Steer Beef)
Broiled Filet Mignon, Fresh Mushrooms

Fresh Vegetables                  Potatoes du Jour

Homemade Pudding   Ice Cream   Sherbet   Assorted Pies
Fried Cream au Rum               Zabaione

Coffee, Tea, Milk, Buttermilk, Iced Tea or Coffee

*"Doc" Puccinelli*
*Proprietaire de Cuisine*

**A curious aspect of the cover of the S.S. *Rex* menu is the use of the crown that is very much the same as the crown logo used by the Italian liner S.S. *Rex* on its printed advertisements.**

the casino and boarded a taxi to return to shore. The waiters called them sea gulls, because "all they do is eat, squawk, shit, and fly."

Despite its many other attractions, the *Rex* existed to entice people to part with their money. To this end, Cornero was not above staffing his ship with shills. Shills were typically attractive young women, occasionally men, who earned five dollars a shift to gamble. At the beginning of a shift, the house gave each shill twenty dollars. Their function was to sit down at any empty game table and begin to play, thus drawing others to join in the action. Any money a shill won belonged to the house, so winnings were kept in plain sight at all times. Pit bosses and croupiers kept an eagle eye on the shills, and knew to a dime how much they won or lost.

The casino was the ship's heart. Music, dining, dancing, drinking, and other entertainment were loss

leaders, provided only to encourage patrons to spend time there. Most would succumb to the temptation to gamble.

At thirty-eight, Cornero was still described as young and good looking, an image he enhanced with meticulous attention to his apparel. One might see him strolling the Santa Monica Pier in an expensive tailored suit, a spotless white Stetson hat, and shoes polished to a high shine. Like the "hardy Piedmontese" he liked to boast about, he had enormous energy—so much, in fact, that he routinely stayed up all night and confined his sleep to short naps during the day. Moreover, he possessed a phenomenal memory, keeping all his accounts in his head and remembering every transaction down to its most minute detail. And he rarely if ever forgot people's names and faces—including those of thousands of casino patrons—even those he encountered only once. He also

Cornero leased the bingo parlor below deck to R. Donen, one of his partners, so its operation was separate from Tony's gambling casino.

On opening night, thousands of people crowded the Santa Monica Pier, all waiting for a chance to ride a water taxi to the *Rex*.

displayed a sentimental streak that was altogether missing from his colleagues in the gambling trade. He invariably carried a full wallet, and freely gave away cash to people he felt were in need. On board the *Rex*, and no doubt before that on the *Tango*, it was not unusual for him to reimburse a distraught wife when he saw that her husband had lost his entire week's salary at the tables.

Even patrons who consistently lost their money at his hands found Cornero likeable. He seasoned his language with colorful slang, referring affectionately to his customers as "squirrels," because, as he explained it, squirrels enjoy getting together to have lots of fun. In fact, in gamblers' lingo, "squirrel" was just another term for "sucker"—but "sucker" was a word Tony loathed.

NOIR AFLOAT

**Water taxis unloaded passengers at Santa Monica Pier.**

Almost all members of gambling syndicates detested publicity, preferred to remain in the shadows, were close-mouthed by nature, and avoided confrontation with authorities, responding to them only through their attorneys. To the contrary, Tony Cornero visibly dominated the Southern California gambling scene, thrived on the publicity he both received and generated, and welcomed the notoriety that resulted from it. Sensing the value of advertising in any form, he was his own publicity agent, as well as that of the *Rex*, and seldom resisted an opportunity to promote both.

# Police Raid *Rex*

On May 13, 1938, only a week after the *Rex* opened for business, the authorities raided the ship. A force of one hundred Santa Monica police, led by the ironically named Chief Charles Dice and by Santa Monica Mayor Edmond Gillette, stormed Santa Monica Pier. Mayor Gillette began the action, bellowing an order that all water taxis were to stay put. Two taxis quickly cast off and headed out to sea. Without a moment's hesitation, forty policemen commandeered one of the taxis still at the pier. Yet another taxi was already half-full of patrons, but was nonetheless commandeered by Officer John Klein (chief criminal investigator for Los Angeles District Attorney Buron Fitts), Captain George Contreras of the Santa Monica police, and Walter Hunter of the sheriff's vice squad. Both taxis sped off to the *Rex*. Deputy District Attorney Tom Cavett and several police waited on the pier.

Despite ten years of efforts to rid the Southern California coast of floating casinos, the leaders of the raid on the *Rex*—Captain Contreras in particular—were unprepared for what occurred when the taxis reached their destination. The first surprise came when the operator of the water taxi carrying the forty police officers refused to tie up to the *Rex* to allow the police to board. Instead, he followed orders from the *Rex*'s crew to turn around and take the unwelcome police back to shore.

Tony Cornero himself appeared on deck to deal with the other water taxi. At first, he declared that only Captain Contreras, whom he knew, could come aboard. When Contreras identified Klein and Dice, Cornero invited all three to join him on the ship for "purposes of discussion," provided there be no interference with the *Rex*'s normal activities. With no police support, the three men had little choice but to accept his terms. The patrons on the commandeered taxi came aboard to play, while Klein, Contreras, and Dice—behind closed doors—began a lengthy and heated debate with Tony over the question of jurisdiction.

Hours later, the argument came to a peaceful end. The three officials accepted Cornero's offer to submit, along with fifteen of his casino employees, to a technical arrest to force a test case. It was of the utmost concern to Tony that the public knew that he had no intention to operate illegally, and that he was both willing and eager to prove to the authorities that he was not doing so. Cornero insisted that both he and Assistant District Attorney Klein issue statements for the press explaining their mutual decision.

*Opposite:* **Captain George Contreras of the sheriff's office, in the white straw fedora, serves an abatement warrant to Fred Grange of the *Rex*. From left, Santa Monica Police Chief Charles Dice, Grange, the ship captain W.J. Stanley, and bingo operator R. Donen.**

NOIR AFLOAT

Police Raid Rex

55
S.S. REX

Accordingly, Klein, on behalf of District Attorney Buron Fitts, prepared a statement:

There has always been a question whether these men are in the confines of Santa Monica Bay or not. They claim they are on the high seas and the only laws that apply are the rules of the sea. We take the position that the three-mile limit extends three miles from an imaginary line drawn from Point Dume on the north to Point Vicente on the south. It is for the courts to determine this question.

In his declaration, Tony depicted himself as fully in control of the situation:

We are submitting to arrest under this technical arrangement to clarify this question once and for all. The reason we sent the officers back, with the exception of Assistant District Attorney Klein, Captain Contreras, and Chief Dice, was because it was a question of finding out the purpose of their visit. We wanted to learn their aims, so we called this conference and made this agreement.

By then, it was well past the ship's usual closing time. As an added sign of his good faith, Tony had already sent the fifteen *Rex* employees to shore in the last water taxi of the evening, and invited Klein, Contreras, and Dice to ride back with him in his private speedboat.

Meanwhile, those in charge at the Santa Monica Pier—waiting several hours with no news on what was transpiring on the *Rex*—became increasingly nervous and inclined to take action. Shortly after midnight, Tom Cavett, a chief investigator for the district attorney, was guarding the dock area when the water taxi *Tornado* tied up and discharged a full load of customers returning from the *Rex*. None indicated that anything unusual had taken place aboard the floating palace. Frustrated, Cavett turned back toward the *Tornado* in time to see her crewman casting off her mooring lines. "Stay put!" he yelled, racing toward the taxi. "You're all under arrest!" When his orders were ignored, Cavett, to the amazement of those watching, threw himself across the bow of the already moving boat.

The *Tornado's* operator revved her engines to full speed, sending the taxi leaping through the water with Cavett hanging on for dear life. Once out of sight of the pier, she slowed enough for the frantic lawman to crawl aboard. Cavett found himself in the company of Tony Cornero's older brother Frank and his friend Ralph Owen. Laughingly, Frank told his bedraggled hostage that the *Tornado* was going "out to the *Rex* to see the boss." Cavett hoped he would soon find out what had happened to Klein, Contreras, and Dice. But the water taxi cruised north as far as Malibu, and then headed back to the pier. Along the way, Cavett was shoved onto an empty boat in the Santa Monica yacht harbor and left to make his own way to the pier. It took him two hours to do so, but once back at the dock he spotted the *Tornado* among the moored taxis, with Frank Cornero and Ralph Owen nearby. Summoning one of the many policemen still patrolling the area, Cavett identified the two of them as "the men who took me to sea" and demanded their immediate arrest. The officer complied, and Frank and his friend were handcuffed, whisked to the Santa Monica jail, and charged with kidnapping.

Ralph Owen, in the straw boater, and Tony Cornero's brother Frank, are arrested for kidnapping after they took Tom Cavett of the district attorney's office on an unexpected boat ride.

At almost the same time, close to 3 A.M., the last water taxi from the *Rex* arrived at the dock. Sheriff's Captain Walter Hunt, still unaware of what had transpired aboard the gambling ship, was fed up with just standing around. Not to be outdone by the bold action of Tom Cavett, he ordered every *Rex* employee aboard the taxi—among them, of course, those selected by Tony for the test case—arrested then and there on charges of violating state gambling laws. In all, sixty-three people were taken to the Santa Monica jail, where they were booked and confined.

When Cornero, Klein, Contreras, and Dice pulled alongside the pier less than a half-hour later, there was no group of fifteen employees on hand to join their boss in subjecting themselves to the agreed-upon courteous technical arrest. Cornero made no attempt to conceal his fury, whereupon, he, too, was arrested. Convinced he had been double-crossed—but not sure by whom—he rushed to a nearby phone to call his attorneys, demanding they come immediately. While waiting for the lawyers, and in the presence of an incredulous police force, Cornero quarreled loudly and uselessly with the D.A.'s men, sheriff's captains, chief of police, and the Santa Monica mayor over what had gone wrong and why. When Cornero learned that his brother had been jailed as well, the decibel level on the pier increased considerably as he dressed down a subdued and exhausted Tom Cavett.

Suddenly, the two water taxis that had quickly taken off from the dock at the start of the raid many hours before returned to shore. One came in and moored at the dock. The other continued cruising nearby while its operator tried to size up the situation. When a policeman shouted to him to tie up his craft, he panicked and headed out to sea. Police drew their guns and began firing. Fifteen bullets sped toward the departing taxi. Two hit the boat itself, and another whizzed by the head of a crewman standing at its gangway opening. Cornero grabbed hold of Chief Dice, insisted that he stop the gunfire, and promised that he would see to it that the miscreant taxi operator turned himself in. Only then did Dice order his officers to cease firing.

Once the gunplay subsided, Cornero's lawyers, who had been waiting at a safe distance, came onto the pier. They responded with a tactic to prevent any further action, one all too familiar to Fitts's deputies and the sheriff's captains. The attorneys sought an injunction to restrain authorities from further interference with

**From left, Tony Cornero, Deputy District Attorney John Klein, Captain George Contreras and Santa Monica Police Chief Charles Dice meet aboard the *Rex*. Cornero agreed to a technical arrest to determine once and for all the exact location of the three-mile limit.**

the *Rex.* Cornero's lawyers took their client in tow, guaranteeing to escort him to jail, where they would make arrangements not only for Cornero, but also for the sixty-three incarcerated *Rex* employees, plus Frank Cornero and Ralph Owen, to be released on bail.

The first of what would become many raids on the *Rex* had been launched by local authorities on Friday the 13th, and bad fortune befell those who carried out the botched raid. On Sunday, May 15, attorneys for Cornero and the McGough brothers called on Superior Court Judge Orlando A. Rhodes at his Santa Monica residence, and were received courteously. After hearing their complaints, Rhodes decided it was unclear who had jurisdiction over the *Rex's* anchorage location, and responded to the lawyers' request for a temporary injunction. His order prohibited city or county officials and their agents from seizing, attacking, or otherwise interfering with operations of the casino, the water taxi company that served her, or the employees of either.

NOIR AFLOAT

Less than an hour later, the *Rex* reopened. Cornero seized the opportunity to hammer home his new-found martyred-businessman image to the public. That evening he held an impromptu press conference on the deck of the *Rex* for visiting reporters, stating:

> We've spent $200,000 to open up out here. Don't think I'm dumb enough not to know where I am! I've sent men to Washington to define this question for me, and I've got a retired U.S. Navy captain, Walter Kirkham, in command of this ship. His word is law out here!

On Monday, May 16, the Santa Monica City Council weighed in. Although there had been no public uproar over the presence of the *Rex*, Council members had, like the mayor, received numerous complaints about her from influential civic leaders in their individual constituencies. The gist was always the same: a floating casino on the city's doorstep was not only a moral danger, it was a threat to the economic and behavioral stability of the community. Emboldened by state and county law enforcement opposition to the *Rex*, the Council abruptly instructed the city attorney to order the McGough brothers to vacate the waiting room on the pier and remove the new dock and gangplanks adjacent to it.

This unilateral foray by the Council brought Mayor Gillette into its chambers on the run. He reminded the council members that they had given the McGoughs permission to use the waiting room and install the dock in the first place, and that the brothers had gone ahead and spent several thousand dollars for renovation, equipment, etc., solely on the basis of the Council's approval. Furthermore, the city was receiving two and a half cents from the McGoughs for each passenger they delivered to and from the *Rex*. To rescind approval now, the mayor ventured to opine, would be acting in bad faith. The Council ignored the warning, ordering the city treasurer to accept no more funds from the McGoughs and to return money already received.

The next day, Cornero attorney A.J. Cleff addressed the Council. Acting on behalf of the McGough brothers, he delivered a forceful reminder that a Superior Court judge's restraining order was still in effect. The Council, he warned, was thus in danger of being found in contempt of court, as well as subject to civil damages, if the court should decide to make the injunction permanent. Chastened,

**Santa Monica Mayor Edmund Gillette and Santa Monica's police chief Charles Dice.**

**Police Raid Rex**

the Council turned its attention to other matters, and taxi service to the *Rex* continued.

On Friday, May 20, a week after their "abduction" of Tom Cavett, Frank Cornero and Ralph Owen appeared in Santa Monica Municipal Court for a hearing on charges against them. Municipal Judge Joseph Chambers dismissed the case, dryly commenting, "I don't believe testimony at this hearing shows that arrests on kidnapping charges were warranted."

On Saturday, May 21, an infuriated District Attorney Buron Fitts petitioned the California Supreme Court for a writ of prohibition against the restraining order of Judge Rhodes, asserting that it interfered with legitimate efforts to enforce the state's anti-gambling statutes. On Monday, May 23, the California justices, aware that a Superior Court hearing on the injunction was pending, chose to deny Fitts's petition. Cornero and his crew appeared to be winning every round of this legal boxing match.

On Tuesday, May 24, a hearing to show cause as to why the temporary injunction against interference with the *Rex* should not be made permanent took place as scheduled in Los Angeles Superior Court, with Judge Orlando Rhodes presiding. At the conclusion of the two-day hearing, Judge Rhodes ruled that the *Rex,* at her present location three and one-half miles from shore, was anchored within the jurisdiction of California, according to the state's Fish and Game Laws (a source not previously used to determine a gambling ship's jurisdictional status). The Judge declared that those laws set an imaginary straight line between Point Dume and Point Vicente as the outer limit of Santa Monica Bay. Only beyond that line, roughly fourteen miles from the Santa Monica shoreline, would a ship be considered as on the "high seas." With that, he dissolved the temporary restraining order.

Immediately, Mayor Gillette ordered Santa Monica harbor guards to arrest any person who attempted to go to the *Rex*, and to see to it that all of the McGoughs' water taxis were anchored behind the Santa Monica breakwater and kept there. Shortly thereafter, the mayor himself once again rode out to the *Rex*. He found her closed, with only a small skeleton crew aboard.

All sixty-three people arrested during the raid on the *Rex*, plus Cornero and the McGoughs, were free on bail. On May 31, five days after Judge Rhodes's decision, they were arraigned in Santa Monica Municipal Court on gambling charges and their trial set for July 19. District Attorney Fitts now had a month to build a case against Cornero and his crew to prove them guilty of breaking state gambling laws.

Meanwhile, in the city of Redondo Beach, nineteen miles south of Santa Monica, but still within the boundaries of Los Angeles County, the following news item was printed:

> Preparations on Monstad Pier, Redondo, for taxi business this summer. . . Though [owner] Captain Monstad is reticent about his plans, it is understood he is arranging for a fleet of fast taxis to ply between Redondo, San Diego, Catalina, Ventura, [and] Santa Monica. . . Waiting room, ticket office, elaborate lighting for night service, electric signs, floodlights, parking places. . . Persons connected with taxis expected to reside in Redondo. . . Café and parking locations being sought. . . Rentals will rise. . . All good business for Redondo.

**Monstad Pier at Redondo Beach is depicted in this photo postcard. Palos Verdes is in the background.**

Captain Monstad had built the pier in 1926. For several years he, his wife Daisy, and their sons Walter and Wilbur operated a fleet of fishing barges off Redondo Beach. The district attorney had a hunch that Captain Monstad was reticent about his plans because the chief beneficiary of the extensive alterations would be Cornero, and the primary to-and-from destination of the taxis would be a gambling ship. Fitts guessed correctly. Cornero had signed an eighteen-year lease covering use of the Monstad Pier, and its new landing facilities.

# *Rex* Moves to Redondo Beach

On June 15, 1938, Cornero towed the *Rex* south and anchored her three and one-half miles off the coast of Redondo Beach. In her new spot, the *Rex* was still anchored between Point Dume and Point Vicente. So, according to Judge Rhodes's recent ruling, the *Rex* was close enough to allow enforcement of applicable gambling laws.

Cornero took out a full-page advertisement in the *Redondo Reflex*, written in the form of an open letter to Redondo Beach residents:

> The S.S. *Rex*, largest and finest vessel of its kind in the world, has shifted its position so as to be nearest of access through Redondo Beach.
>
> In order that the residents of your community may gain some idea as to the magnitude and importance of this move and its direct effect upon your welfare and comfort, the following information is respectfully submitted.
>
> To begin with, the operators of the S.S. *Rex* are highly appreciative of the splendid spirit of cooperation and friendliness exhibited by the business men and residents of Redondo Beach. Our type of business has operated successfully and continuously off the coast of Long Beach for more than ten and one-half years. Ours is a year-round business.
>
> We employ some 260 men, whose average income should exceed $10.00 per day. These employees have been carefully selected, are for the most part family men, and represent a type of individual that is an asset to any community. They are all required to become residents of Redondo Beach or the South Bay area within the next 30 days.
>
> All supplies, commodities, and other items essential to the operation of the S.S. *Rex* will be purchased from merchants in Redondo Beach.
>
> Our total payroll and local purchases should exceed $100,000 per month. We are informed that this represents the largest sum ever expended locally by any single enterprise in the history of Redondo Beach.
>
> The daily attendance on our vessel will approximate some 1,200 to 2,000 persons during the week and should well exceed 3,000 on Saturdays, Sundays, and holidays. These

**Opposite: Advertisements promoted the *Rex* as the most elegant and exciting gambling ship ever to be anchored in Redondo Beach.**

NOIR AFLOAT

**Rex Moves to Redondo Beach**

visitors are almost entirely tourists or residents of such communities as Beverly Hills, Hollywood, Malibu Beach, Pasadena, and other prosperous areas.

Carefully compiled statistics show that in addition to the above figures each visitor will expend an average of 50 cents in this community over and above parking and other charges incidental to a visit to our vessel. Thus, when our vessel entertains 3,000 visitors, Redondo Beach is virtually assured of $1,500 in new money over and above the daily expenditure by the vessel itself.

We are of the firm opinion that despite the current business recession, the presence of the S.S. *Rex* off the coast of Redondo Beach will result in this city becoming a white spot on the business map of California. Why? Because we are spending approximately $3,000 each week with radio stations and metropolitan newspapers, in telling seven million people of the attractions of Redondo Beach.

(Signed) _____

S.S. *Rex*

The *Rex* began operations that month. Patrons materialized by the thousands, just as quickly as they had when she opened in Santa Monica. Cornero maintained a steady flow of advertising and promotion, including "*Rex*-o-Grams" in local papers publicizing not only his ship, but also the annual Redondo Rodeo and Carnival and other South Bay events.

Although Tony announced that the ship maintained an on-board bankroll of seventy-five thousand dollars to pay off bets and an operating expense fund of twenty-five thousand dollars in local banks, he kept the amount of her profits a closely guarded secret. When questioned about them, he invariably bristled: "Those stories about the *Rex* making a fortune every week are so much hogwash. Of every dollar played across our boards, 98.6 cents goes back to the customers." Elaborating further, he told reporters his daily cost of operations was six thousand dollars, "with 350 employees getting one-half that amount in wages. So we are an asset to the merchants. We make money circulate!"

Nevertheless, it was obvious the ship was making vast amounts of money. More than one observant reporter spotted Cornero, accompanied by burly guards—even an occasional policeman—bringing money ashore in suitcases for deposit in area banks. At the time, casinos' medium of exchange was more often silver dollars than paper currency. The coins were used both as chips and for paying off winners. Indeed, during the *Rex*'s brief stay in Santa Monica, one local bank had told Cornero that if he expected them to handle his account, he would have to buy a truck to transport his heavy deposits.

On July 19, Superior Court proceedings in the case of Anthony Cornero Stralla *et al.* began and ended with the announcement that the trial would be postponed until November. Newspaper reports did not indicate any reason for this decision. Frustrated with the further delays, District Attorney Fitts secured a grand jury indictment charging Cornero with a new set of charges: felony bookmaking aboard the *Rex* the night of the Santa

NOIR AFLOAT

Monica raid. Undercover police sent to the *Rex* prior to the Santa Monica raid had reported an off-track betting facility at the far end of the casino, the first of its kind in the gambling ship trade. That fact had been lost sight of, however, when the initial attempt to raid the ship turned into a complete debacle on the Santa Monica Pier. Before the day was out, both men were arrested. Cornero's attorney, Arthur Verge, after arranging for their release on bail, informed the press that they would be arraigned the following week, and the *Rex* would close down in the meantime. The *Rex*, however, remained open during this period.

Cornero, perhaps in a strategic effort to justify not closing the *Rex* down, had a law firm representing his Nevada corporation, Rex, Inc., petition the U.S. District Court of Appeals for a writ of prohibition against any further interference on the part of local authorities. Because the *Rex* operated under a charter that was granted by Nevada and was "signed on the high seas," the petition argued, she was subject only to the laws of the State of Nevada and of the United States, and not those of California or any of its localities.

On July 25, 1938, Cornero and Adams appeared in Superior Court before Judge Clarence Kincaid for arraignment on the felony bookmaking charge. To no one's surprise, they pleaded not guilty on grounds that the *Rex* had at the time—and indeed continued to be—outside state jurisdiction. Trial was set for September 15.

Not content with the pending charges on bookmaking, and concerned that Rex, Inc.'s petition for a writ of prohibition against further interference with the ship on grounds the state lacked jurisdiction over her would be granted, District Attorney Fitts went ahead and planned another raid.

At 7:45 P.M. on Wednesday, September 7, Fitts and Contreras, plus one hundred deputy sheriffs and district attorney's investigators, assembled at Redondo Beach's Monstad Pier, boarded two launches, and headed for the *Rex*. Tony must have been tipped off, because the gambling ship was already under tow seaward and somewhat northward by the tug *Milton S. Patrick*. Being mid-week, only a few hundred patrons were aboard. As the launches approached, they were deluged by streams of water plied by crewmen from the *Rex*'s high-pressure hoses. Other hands on deck threateningly wielded baseball bats in anticipation of any boarding attempt. In the casino, Tony took assured his patrons that nothing more than a little friendly horseplay was occurring outside—nothing worth leaving the tables for.

The crew's efforts to repel the raiders failed. Once within hailing distance, Fitts shouted to the tug's captain to drop the tow and to Cornero to drop anchor and allow the officers to come aboard. Failure to obey, he yelled, would be responded to with tear gas. The tug cut loose, and the big ship's descending anchor chains rattled loudly as her crew complied with Tony's order to do as the D.A. ordered. Fitts himself remained in the launch, sending Contreras and Deputy District Attorney Klein onto the deck of the *Rex*, not to negotiate this time, but to deliver a strict ultimatum. Contreras told Tony that unless he and his key staff submitted to arrest then and there, "the district attorney will set up a blockade and starve you out, and if that doesn't work, we'll sink the ship!" Cornero, temporarily cornered and mindful of his patrons, promptly surrendered. He and nine members of the ship's staff were arrested and taken into custody.

Deputies and agents confiscated numerous items of gambling paraphernalia and lowered them over the ship's sides into the waiting launches. Water taxis, which had been curiously and cautiously following the

**Like a beacon that could be seen from shore, the *Rex* lit up the night sea with bright lights and red neon illuminating the full length of the roof of the casino.**

raiding party, were hailed alongside to carry the stunned patrons back to shore. Fitts then ordered the tug captain to set up his towline and haul the *Rex* further seaward, to a point no fewer than ten miles from the Redondo Beach Pier, and leave her there.

Cornero and the nine employees were taken to the Redondo Beach Police Court, booked on charges of gambling violations, and released on bail—paid by Tony in the amount of one hundred dollars for himself and twenty-five dollars for each of the others. Arraignment was set for September 12. For want of more appropriate space, the gambling paraphernalia was stored in the women's section of the Redondo Beach police station.

Two days later, while the district attorney and the sheriff's captain were still congratulating themselves on having at last closed down Cornero's operation, the *Rex* reopened for business, a full twelve miles from shore. Although tossing a bit in the rougher waters, she was anchored strongly enough to be boarded safely from the water taxis. Despite of the much longer ride, an undiminished stream of customers continued to flow from Redondo Beach to the floating palace, whose undaunted and ebullient owner now posted highly visible notices on the Monstad Pier—and published them in the local press:

> OPERATORS OF THE *REX* ARE HIGHLY APPRECIATIVE OF THE SPLENDID SPIRIT OF CO-OPERATION AND FRIENDLINESS EXHIBITED BY THE BUSINESSMEN AND RESIDENTS OF REDONDO BEACH. OUR TYPE OF BUSINESS HAS OPERATED SUCCESSFULLY AND CONTINUOUSLY OFF THE COAST OF LONG BEACH [sic] FOR MORE THAN TEN AND ONE-HALF YEARS!

District Attorney Buron Fitts realized that in preparing his prosecution, he would need to carefully consider the fact that the *Rex* had been moving under tow at the time of the raid. He realized that the ship's location, rather than the nature of the crimes charged, would be the focus of the defense. Cornero's attorneys would probably argue that the *Rex* had been outside the three-mile limit. The outcome of the case would then turn on where that three-mile limit was.

The whole problematic issue of "open seas," however, might just be avoided if, given the curve of the shoreline, the under-tow *Rex* had by chance been *less than* three miles from land at the moment of the raid. Careful calculations resulted in no such good fortune, but they did reveal that the ship had dropped anchor on command at a point exactly 3.7 miles out from Hermosa Beach, the little city immediately to the north of Redondo Beach. Accordingly, after informing Cornero's lawyers of this fact, Fitts had the case transferred to Hermosa Beach.

Arraignment took place as scheduled on September 12, in Hermosa Beach Municipal Court. All ten defendants pleaded not guilty to five misdemeanor gambling charges, and trial was set for September 16. When the day arrived, no fewer than fifty-six conscientious citizens made up the jury pool. To their considerable disappointment, however, Tony and the other defendants waived the jury trial they had originally requested.

Cornero's attorney, Samuel Rummel, told Municipal Court Judge Collamer Bridge that he would not deny that gambling took place on the *Rex*; he would contend that the court lacked jurisdiction, because the ship had been operating beyond the three-mile limit, at 3.61 miles from the nearest shore point. The prosecutor, Deputy District Attorney Thomas O'Brien, argued that the waters in which the *Rex* was anchored were part of Santa Monica Bay, where the three-mile limit was not three miles from shore, but three miles from an imaginary straight line between Point Dume and Point Vicente, the headlands of Santa Monica Bay. To be beyond that limit, the *Rex* would have to have been more than ten miles from the coast. O'Brien cited numerous precedents in support of his argument, the most recent being the decision of Judge Rhodes in Los Angeles Superior Court.

After a deputy county surveyor corroborated O'Brien's description of the *Rex*'s location, Rummel called his chief witness to the stand, and Cornero finally had his day in court. In a display of amiable confidence, Cornero explained to Judge Bridge that he had been connected with and on the seas since the age of fourteen. He stressed his extensive study of the California coastline. Turning to history, he declared that never on any of the many maps drawn since the first explorers of California—not even on the charts of Juan Cabrillo—had the area the prosecuting attorney was referring to as Santa Monica Bay been so described. "A bay," he went on, "is a body of water protected from the elements and where mariners may seek shelter and provisions." Moreover, the body of water in question was wider at its mouth than at its base, and thus accurately mapped and charted as open sea.

Following this, and testifying for the defense, the city attorney of Redondo Beach described the many losses sustained annually by boat owners in this unprotected area. Further, a marine insurance underwriter testified to the insurance he had personally sold to numerous local boat owners, adding that in fixing rates, his company ruled the area as open sea and not as a protected bay.

At the end of the day, Judge Bridge indicated he would take all testimony under consideration and render his decision in five working days. Debriefing his team, Buron Fitts realized how much the status quo had changed. Over years of gambling-ship trials, he had become accustomed to taciturn and frequently surly casino operators, who answered as few questions as possible and left it entirely up to their lawyers to defend them. Anthony Cornero Stralla was prepared to speak for himself in court.

On September 23, Judge Bridge announced that there was no such entity as Santa Monica Bay, and that beyond three miles from shore, the waters between Point Dume and Point Vicente constituted a portion of the open sea, over which only the United States government held jurisdiction:

> In this case, the distance between Point Vicente and Point Dume is twenty-nine miles. There is no point landward from said points where the distance from shore to shore exceeds twenty-seven miles; the area appears to offer no protection or shelter to ships, and the whole area is obviously a portion of the open sea.

With that, the case was dismissed. The *Rex* was promptly towed back to her original Redondo Beach location, slightly more than three miles off Monstad Pier, where she continued to draw capacity crowds, much to the satisfaction of the local merchants and chamber of commerce.

Shortly thereafter, the *Los Angeles Times* reported that attorneys for Rex, Inc. had sought a dismissal of their petition for a writ prohibiting raids against the ship by Los Angeles County authorities. U.S. District Judge Henry Holzer, who had had the petition under consideration, granted the dismissal without prejudice, thus leaving the authorities free to file a similar action in the future. By now, Tony considered himself as much involved with the judicial system as he was with the *Rex*. Buoyed by what he felt his personal success in convincing the Hermosa Beach court that state jurisdiction ended three miles from shore, Cornero planned to be his own chief witness in Superior Court, as well. Cornero viewed himself as engaged in hand-to-hand combat with Buron Fitts. He intended to personally battle the district attorney, one round after another, all the way to the California Supreme Court.

The superior court trial to consider the charges of illegal bookmaking was held the following Monday, September 26. Los Angeles Superior Court Judge Frank Smith presided, and this time a jury would be deciding the outcome. Deputy District Attorney Thomas O'Brien again took up the cudgels for the prosecution. One sheriff's deputy after another testified convincingly that he had observed and, acting as an undercover agent, actually placed bets in a full-blown bookmaking operation aboard the *Rex* while she was anchored four miles off Santa Monica. The defense made no effort to refute the testimony. Instead, Cornero's attorneys made it clear that the issue was whether the state had any right to interfere.

Prosecutor O'Brien curtly informed the jury that a ship would have to be anchored over three miles "beyond the mouth" of any bay on the California coast in order to be outside the state's territorial waters. To the surprise of Cornero's counsel, he then asked and received permission to display (and designate as Exhibit A) a map on which the waters off Santa Monica were clearly labeled "Santa Monica Bay."

NOIR AFLOAT

Defense attorneys countered with numerous other cartographic depictions of the area, ranging from ancient to modern and in no instance bearing any identification of a bay. The defense then asked its star witness to take the stand. Modestly describing himself as a self-qualified expert on the history of the California coast, Cornero expounded at length and in a friendly and informative manner on how both Cabrillo and Vizcaino and all the other explorers who came after them had realized that the inlet opposite Santa Monica was merely a bight—a curve or recess in the coastline, neither sheltering nor protected from the elements, and in no way identifiable as a bay enclosed by headlands. When confronted by O'Brien with a map bearing the words "Santa Monica Bay," he dismissed the description as merely a mapmaker's error.

At the close of testimony, Judge Smith declared that he would decide whether the *Rex* had been anchored within state jurisdiction on the night in question. He instructed the jurors to accept his decision as a fact during their deliberations. When the trial resumed, the judge announced his opinion that the waters off Santa Monica were indeed part of a bay. A subdued and solemn Tony Cornero threw himself on the mercy of the court. Given permission to address the jury, he respectfully accepted the judge's decision and, in sorrowful tones, acknowledged that the conclusion he himself had so carefully arrived at was erroneous, and he hoped that the good members of the panel would believe he had made an honest mistake. In their closing statement to the jury, his lawyers leaned hard on the concept of no criminal intent:

> If you believe that Anthony Cornero Stralla was sincere in his belief that he was outside the
> state and [that] he desired to violate no law, then you should acquit him.

The jurors deliberated late into the night, finally informing Judge Smith that they were hopelessly deadlocked ten to two for acquittal. He abruptly dismissed them and ordered a retrial, which was docketed for November 14, some six weeks away.

Cornero would have preferred a verdict of guilty. If he were found guilty, his attorneys would have immediately appealed the decision. Cornero was confident that if not the next higher court, then the one above it would vindicate his claim to be operating in the open seas. Moreover, while the *Rex* could have continued to function pending the outcome of an appeal, in the present situation Fitts could legally continue to keep her closed pending outcome of the retrial. For once, the gregarious proprietor of the floating palace left the court without issuing a statement to the press, leaving District Attorney Buron Fitts to enlighten waiting reporters.

The owners of the *Rex*, Fitts announced, have "yielded to the law, and will cease operations in Santa Monica Bay, at least for the winter." Southern California in those years could count on a steady succession of heavy rains and generally inclement weather from November through March, and Fitts didn't mention that Tony had already planned to close down the *Rex* during that period.

# Return to Santa Monica

On March 18, 1939, the District Appeals Court ruled that Santa Monica Bay was a part of the high seas. Tony immediately made plans to bring the *Rex* back to Santa Monica.

He learned that an anti-gambling-ship petition was being circulated in Santa Monica for presentation to the City Council. To counter it, he hired men to circulate a petition in favor of the *Rex* returning to Santa Monica. At its meeting, the City Council received 250 signatures against the *Rex* returning and 4,900 in favor. City Commissioner T.D. Plumer calmed the distraught council members by informing them they could ignore the pro-*Rex* petition because everyone who signed it had received ten cents for doing so.

He went on to assure the Council that "if we can't prevent the barge from anchoring in the bay, we will at least do our best to prevent them [the operators] from landing or taking off patrons in Santa Monica." Santa Monica Commissioner of Public Works W.W. "Tex" Milliken chimed in with, "They won't land on the municipal pier." Mayor Gillette contented himself with a summary: "The commissioners are unanimous in the position that the gambling ship operators must be prevented from using municipal property in any way."

On March 27, 1939, the *Evening Outlook* reported that the gambling ship *Rex* was expected to arrive in Santa Monica Bay within a few days. She dropped anchor three and one-half miles straight out from Santa Monica Pier on March 28.

On March 30, the *Rex* opened for business, with six water taxis providing ferry service to and from the renovated boat landing. The X (symbolic of *Rex*) Water Taxi Company—in reality Frank Haskell, who had been part of water taxi operations for Southern California gambling ships since the 1920s—was her transportation lifeline.

Haskell did not own the taxi boats. He hired shore-boat owners from other parts of the coast to work for his company. Each taxi operator was paid $7.50 an hour while hauling passengers, and $2.50 an hour whenever he was on standby. Each twenty-five-cent fare went to the gambling ship and, given Tony's way of doing things, ten per cent of the gross take was turned over to the city. Haskell appeared on the landing deck weekly, brandishing a cigar box full of cash, from which he paid each taxi operator the amount due him. Santa Monica officials were certain Haskell's operation was in no way independent of Tony Cornero, but they could not prove it.

On duty twenty-four hours a day, the boat owners made considerable money, as did the marine gas

*Opposite:* **In 1938, water taxis operated from the end of the lower deck of at Santa Monica Pier, carrying passengers to and from the Rex.**

**Return to Santa Monica**

station owner on Santa Monica Pier who fueled their craft. Each powered by two Chrysler engines, the taxis were sleek, fast (thirty-five miles per hour or more), state-of-the-art vessels, complete with canvas tops to keep out ocean spray and exhaust fumes—the latter being toxic enough to nauseate anyone breathing them.

Horse race betting continued on the *Rex* as well. Shore-side bookmakers not only resented that Cornero was directly competing with them, but had no idea how he was managing to do it. The lifeline for bookmaking was rapid and reliable telephone communication with the racetracks. There was no phone line to the *Rex*. Other bookies wondered how he could get track results as fast—sometimes even faster—than they themselves could.

Cornero's secret was a medical device called a diathermy machine, ordinarily used to generate short-wave radio signals to therapeutically heat the human body. Procuring one of these marvels, he had it installed at a secret site and equipped with an antenna and reflector aimed directly at the floating casino. Race results communicated via Morse code using the diathermy transmitter flew straight to the *Rex*. The system worked flawlessly until police located the transmitter site and smashed the equipment.

Undaunted, Tony devised an alternate scheme. He had a telephone installed at an undisclosed location on the pier, perhaps in some rarely frequented area of one of the numerous small cafes, bait shops, or boat rental outlets that lined it. He had long since established friendly relations with pier proprietors, all of whom liked him and none of whom were predisposed to help to the police. Then he purchased four and one-half miles of standard-sized telephone cable and had it installed along a circuitous route from the phone on the pier to another on the *Rex*. The cable was held underwater by twenty-pound weights tied to it every five hundred feet. "Trackmen" for the *Rex* called in race results to the pier phone, answered by an always ready-and-waiting Cornero employee, who would in turn relay them to the ship. Frequently, the trackmen would be working in tandem with observers equipped with high-powered binoculars and stationed in tall palm trees overlooking the racetrack. From their lofty perches, the numbers of the winning horses would be signaled down as they crossed the finish line.

True to form, Cornero had taken steps to ensure the legality of installing his own telephone line in the Pacific Ocean. He applied for a permit from the United States War Department. That body merely returned his application, explaining that an underwater connection of such length would be unworkable. When his functioning cable was eventually discovered and reported to the Army Corps of Engineers, Cornero promptly re-applied. The matter was given a hearing in Washington, D.C., and the War Department determined that the installation posed no problems of a navigational nature. Not only would the requested permit be approved, but the applicant would not be penalized for having installed it without one. The news release issued by the Department—and reproduced in Los Angeles area papers—indicated that had any objectors been present at the hearing, the decision might have been different. This was a considerable annoyance to the newly established anti-*Rex* troika of Fitts, Contreras, and California Attorney General Warren, who would have readily sent representatives to Washington for the purpose, had they known what Cornero was up to.

*Opposite:* Large posters were displayed in drinking establishments throughout Santa Monica.

WORLD'S *Greatest Casino*

S.S. REX

REX REX

*Race Results Daily*
WE PAY TRACK ODDS

12 MIN. BY X WATER TAXI
FROM
SANTA MONICA PIER
OPEN 24 HOURS A DAY

73
S.S. REX

# A Public Nuisance

On June 7, 1939 the California Supreme Court commenced its hearing of the Los Angeles district attorney's counter appeal to the district court ruling that the *Rex* was outside both state and county jurisdiction. It granted both the defense and prosecution more time to file rebuttal briefs, noting that once briefs were received the Court would have ninety days to render its decision.

California Attorney General Earl Warren viewed the gambling ships as evil incarnate, and their elimination as a moral imperative. Moreover, having already moved their eradication to the top of his professional agenda, he did not intend to sacrifice his political momentum to the leisurely pace of the California Supreme Court. Accordingly, he decided to get rid of all four floating casinos—the *Rex* and the *Texas* at Santa Monica, and the *Tango* and the *Mount Baker* at Long Beach—as soon as possible, and without reference either to the state's jurisdictional limits or to its anti-gambling laws. He considered it necessary to go after all four ships at once because, he said, to raid only one would leave him open to accusations of putting one out of business to benefit the others.

The logistical difficulty of such an all-out effort had lessened somewhat since the hearing before the State Supreme Court. Immediately after the Fourth of July holiday, the *Tango* upped anchor and was towed back to her former anchorage off Long Beach, where she reopened not far from the *Mount Baker*. At sundown on July 7, the *Texas* dropped anchor near the *Rex*. Now renamed for the seventh time, it was none other than the original *La Playa Ensenada*. Like the *Tango* before her, the *Texas* used the Ocean Park Pier waiting room and water taxis. Thus, whatever operational plan Warren came up with would involve only sites off Long Beach and Santa Monica.

Warren was fully aware that he risked severe criticism by acting against the casinos before the Supreme Court determined whether they lay within the state's jurisdiction. Ironically, he was gambling on precedent to protect him—courts had ruled that local authorities could abate a nuisance no matter where it originated.

Earl Warren appointed the young and energetic Warren Olney III as chief of the criminal division of the California attorney general's office. He gave Olney a difficult first assignment: the need to get rid of all four gambling ships operating off the Southern California coast had reached crisis proportions. It was Olney's responsibility, he went on, to come up with a way to bring their operations to a complete and permanent halt—the

*Opposite:* **Gamblers gathered around the dice table on the *Rex*.**

NOIR AFLOAT

A Public Nuisance

sooner, the better. The attorney general promised Olney the full support and assistance of the new chief investigator, Oscar Jahnsen, formerly of the Alameda County district attorney's office, which had proven so valuable that Warren had brought him along to the state level.

Since the attorney general's staff included no maritime lawyers, Olney's first step was to inquire discreetly whether closing the ships would create any legal problems with the federal government. To his great satisfaction, Vice Admiral Stanley Parker of the U.S. Coast Guard, himself a lawyer, announced his opinion that the gambling ships were an "abomination," and enthusiastically approved the strategy Olney described. The United States attorney for the Southern District, Ben Harrison, also reassured him that Warren's plans would not cause conflict with any federal law.

Olney and Jahnsen now got to work on planning, while Earl Warren, in his public appearances, ratcheted his anti-gambling rhetoric to new heights, emphasizing the word "nuisance," and alternating between economic and moral persuasion, depending on his audience. For example, chambers of commerce would be likely to hear him pragmatically characterize the gambling ships as "a great nuisance, which is drawing millions of dollars annually from legitimate trade channels." On the other hand, for the benefit of less monetarily focused listeners, he would wax supremely eloquent, as he had in his brief for the Supreme Court case:

> . . . It would dim the light that shines from the eyes of the Goddess of Justice to hold that the state may guard its citizens from personal injury, may prevent damage to their property, and at the same time is impotent to prohibit acts that impair their morals, deprive them of their character, and induce them to lead idle and dissolute lives. The character of a state depends upon the character of the individuals constituting it.

The Warren team operated under a number of unproven assumptions. They were convinced that *without exception* each of the gambling ships belonged to criminal syndicates and was backed up by dirty money, although they were never able to discover the identity of the underworld figures who owned them. In fact, the *Texas* syndicate did include one or two Mafia associates, and the *Tango's* probably included a former notorious rumrunner ("Doc" Schouweiler, who had served his time in federal prison for that activity), as well as a few local gambling czars. The *Mount Baker*, however, was the product of small-time Long Beach pool hall and real estate entrepreneurs. As for the *Rex*, the most successful of them all, there is no record that it was ever controlled by anyone other than the loquacious and visible Tony Cornero. Warren chose to describe Cornero as the worst of the lot.

The attorney general and Olney suspected that efforts of both Los Angeles District Attorney Fitts and Sheriff Biscailuz to close down the casinos were less than serious. They viewed the repetitively unsuccessful pattern of raids, injunctions, lawsuits, court trials, and appeals over the past ten years as evidence of collusion. In line with that assumption, they now determined to be less than candid with the pair about their new plan. Had Warren not needed the personnel both Fitts and Biscailuz could provide to carry out enforcement action, he would have eliminated them altogether. Further, Warren was convinced that the police departments of both

NOIR AFLOAT

Santa Monica and Long Beach were, as he put it, "subservient to" the gambling ship operators.

The aspect of the "public nuisance" approach that troubled the attorney general, however, was how to avoid the usual abatement route, which was via the injunction process and the inevitable lengthy lawsuit that followed. Olney solved this problem by calling Warren's attention to the statute's inclusion and definition of "the remedy of summary abatement:"

> Once a public nuisance was clearly established, public authorities could move in on, take over, and physically abate the nuisance without seeking an injunction against its perpetrator. Thereafter, the perpetrator could go to court to litigate his right to operate the nuisance, but could not operate it while such litigation was in process.

Olney warned his boss that, given the presence of firearms aboard and their assumption that the ships' operators would not hesitate to use them, going for "summary abatement" would involve greater risk and less certainty of success. Moreover, sizeable numbers of personnel from a variety of local law enforcement agencies would be needed. Nevertheless, the attorney general unhesitatingly opted for it.

By mid-July, Olney and Jahnsen had worked out a strategic plan. In the course of doing so, they had come to understand that the attorney general intended to reach his desired ends by duplicitous means. He would inform the Los Angeles district attorney and sheriff that the gambling ships were a nuisance to the entire state and that he had decided to serve them with abatement notices. But for the present, he would make no mention at all of his decision to take summary abatement action, thus preventing any possibility of a leak to the ship operators that might prompt them to initiate preventive measures. Accordingly, a conference with Fitts and Biscailuz was scheduled to take place in the attorney general's Los Angeles office, during the course of which the abatement notices would be drawn up and arrangements made to simply deliver them to each of the four ships, as well as their taxi operators. Warren of course knew that so mild an action would not motivate the ships' managers to close down, but he felt it was worth giving them a chance to do so voluntarily and, more important, they could not later claim they had been taken by surprise.

By that time, it had become obvious to those interested in the subject that Los Angeles officials were being upstaged in the gambling ship drama. Buron Fitts, who had established for himself a national reputation as an activist, no-nonsense prosecutorial protector of the public good, was no longer the lead player. Earl Warren had taken center stage.

Mayor Bowron decided it would be prudent to take a few well-publicized steps to remind the public of his continued dedication to its welfare. Since the new attorney general was making headlines by denouncing the gambling vessels and all who aided or abetted their operation, he promptly wrote a letter to Earl Warren, fervently praising his efforts and pledging not only his full support, but the services of the entire Los Angeles police force, should that be needed. Warren kept the letter, knowing he could use it later.

Los Angeles police in Venice, directly south of Santa Monica, promptly swarmed off on a sign-hunting expedition, which netted them no fewer than twenty large metal creations, each bearing only a big S.S. *REX* and white arrow pointing in her direction. They carried them all to the Venice police station, labeled them "found property held as evidence," and stored them away.

Santa Monica police, however, were less energetic and decidedly less interested. They did spot several signs bearing a "T" (for the *Texas*) and others showing simply "X" (for the *Rex*). Unsure of the legality of removing them, because they were located on private property, the police returned to base to study the matter. Other than arresting two men caught on the Santa Monica-Ocean Park boardwalk passing out handbills for both the *Rex* and the *Texas*, they did nothing further.

With summer well underway, the *Rex* and her less luxurious counterparts were doing better than ever. Thousands of sailors from Long Beach (and even San Diego) naval installations were patronizing them. Hundreds of thousands of tourists were now flowing into and out of Southern California, and, for many, a visit to a floating casino was a must.

Because of news reports about Congress holding hearings on a bill regarding the gambling ships, many Southern Californians began to wonder if the opportunity to enjoy the floating casinos would be available much longer. Paradoxically, locals who had not yet visited them, but had always meant to do so, began significantly increasing the *Rex's* already spectacular thirty-thousand-a-week attendance. So Cornero felt he could relax a bit, although he continued to see the handwriting on the wall. As for Earl Warren, the delay in passage of the bill caused him no concern. He was within days of carrying out his summary abatement plan. He had no more intended to wait for Congress than he had intended to wait for the Supreme Court.

Toward the fourth week of July 1939, Earl Warren and his top staffers Warren Olney and Oscar Jahnsen arrived in Los Angeles from Sacramento and moved into the attorney general's suite in that city's State Building for what was obviously more than a few days' visit.

In fact, although he was ready to move against the gambling fleet, Warren had not yet shared that with the local officials. He contacted District Attorney Fitts and Sheriff Biscailuz and asked that they and their key deputies meet with him about the floating casinos. Although they fully recognized the advantages of the public nuisance approach, as Warren explained it to them, Fitts and Biscailuz flatly refused his request for the manpower necessary to go after the ships while the California Supreme Court was still in process of determining their jurisdictional status.

The attorney general sensed the time had come to play his ace. He produced the letter from Los Angeles Mayor Bowron, in which the mayor had promised that his police department would provide whatever manpower Warren might need in his efforts to do away with offshore gambling.

Well aware of Bowron's reputation for integrity, both the district attorney and the sheriff were quick to visualize what headlines would result if they refused to help the popular new California attorney general and the Los Angeles mayor in their all-out effort to do away with the "ships from hell." They did not doubt that Warren would take up the mayor on his offer, but he would make certain every Southern California voter knew why he

*Opposite:* Eager customers waited to board a water taxi at Santa Monica Pier.

NOIR AFLOAT

A Public Nuisance

79
S.S. REX

had been compelled to do so. Reluctantly, they cooperated.

The owners of each ship would be formally presented with an abatement notice, which would list the specific reasons why their operations constituted a public nuisance, request them to abate that nuisance, and warn that failure on their part to comply with that request would constitute cause for court action.

On July 28, local newspapers printed the reasons Attorney General Warren declared the gambling ships a public nuisance:

EARL WARREN SERVES NOTICE ON OPERATORS TO ABATE PUBLIC NUISANCE
[The gambling barge herein identified:]
1. Induces people to lead an idle and dissolute life.
2. Induces people of limited means to spend on gambling money necessary for maintenance and support of their minor children and parents and throws said dependents on county and state for support, thereby increasing tax burden of people of California. It is contributing to delinquency of minors of many families by depriving them of necessary support of their parents and by openly glorifying illegal gambling in their eyes.
3. Induces people to neglect their lawful obligations and to squander their money on games prohibited by the constitution and laws of California.
4. It has on many occasions caused people of trust to embezzle money to play at nefarious gambling games.
5. It causes citizens of California to lose their regular employment because of the idle and dissolute habits encouraged by unlawful activities.
6. It attracts pickpockets, bunco men, thieves, racketeers, gangsters, gunmen, and other law violators to the State of California to the detriment of law and order.
7. It has caused the operation of similar gambling ships. There are now four vessels of the same character anchored off the mainland of Los Angeles County—each aggravating the effect of the nuisance and all encouraged by the fabulous profits of illegal activities.

To begin his race against time, Olney focused on what worried him most, which was how to prevent the gambling ships from leaving the area once they were physically taken over and shut down. Left alone, they would certainly steal away to various other locations off the coast and resume business as usual while the inevitable litigation took its snail's-pace course. Olney wanted the ships towed into port and kept there, under guard.

Frustration set in almost immediately. Finding a towing outfit big enough to have four tugs available on a standby arrangement was difficult. When Olney finally located one and swore its owner to secrecy as to what the four tugs were to be used for, the owner informed him it was going to be impossible to get his union crews to help close the gambling ships, since those ships employed union men. Maritime union rules forbade such action. Olney decided the problem was insurmountable, and that the only way to prevent the ships from escaping was to cut their anchor cables, let them drift, and count on the Coast Guard to consider them hazards

to navigation and take charge of bringing them in.

Olney had good reason for not checking with the Guard in advance. Attorney General Warren had long since placed a wiretap on Tony Cornero's phone. It had provided nothing incriminating, but it proved that Tony enjoyed extremely friendly relations with numerous local Coast Guard commanders, as well as with the maritime union, no small number of area businessmen, and even certain religious leaders in the vicinity.

Cutting the vessels loose would present yet another obstacle. Their anchors were huge, tremendously expensive, and not expendable. The *Rex* alone had four of them. Somehow, their location would have to be marked, so they could later be hauled up to the surface. Olney found a waterfront establishment whose proprietor agreed to complete overnight his order for numerous floats in the form of old empty oil drums with rings welded to each and cables attached to each ring. Olney's intent was that the cable could be attached to an anchor chain below the point where the chain was cut. The drum would then rise to the surface and bob about, signaling the anchor's location below. Nor did he forget that at least some of the anchors would have steel cables that could only be cut by a welding torch. He arranged to have crews of welders standing by, ready to head to sea when summoned.

**A Fish and Game boat circled the *Rex* all night to be certain no one boarded or left the ship. Cornero, feeling sorry for the men on board, tossed them bottles of his best scotch to keep their spirits up.**

The next set of decisions involved how to dispose of the expected large sums of money they would find not only on the gaming tables, but in the ships' security cages and safes. In each instance, it would all have to be immediately collected and carefully counted under the eye of the ship's manager, who would then be given a receipt for the full amount. The money itself would be bagged, taken ashore, and deposited in a bank vault. To avoid any possible accusation of mishandling or stealing, Olney decided each boarding force would include two Price Waterhouse accountants to handle those financial tasks. Accordingly, he contacted that firm and, within the hour, received a list of eight accountants, along with instructions on how to reach them when the need arose.

The local facility of the California Fish and Game Commission possessed four patrol boats and crews to man them. As seaworthy craft, the boats were not only of generous size, but fast and easily maneuverable. With one of them, plus four rented independent water taxis for each gambling ship, Olney would have what he needed. Earl Warren had assured him the Commission would put both its boats and crews at his disposal for what it considered a worthy cause. But when Olney contacted its operations office, he was told they would not be able to assist. What had been overlooked was the fact that the boats and crews were authorized only to enforce the fish and game laws, and were insured only to the extent of that specific activity.

To resolve this impasse, Olney proposed that the Office of the Attorney General charter the boats from the Fish and Game Commission. The attorney general's office would secure an additional insurance policy to cover both boats and crews while they were under that charter. The Fish and Game administrators agreed.

Having located and reserved—with hefty down payments to their owners—sixteen independent water taxis for a temporarily unspecified date and assignment, Olney then reported to Earl Warren that their only remaining need was two hundred officers and/or deputies.

On July 31, 1939, Warren returned to Fitts and Biscailuz. They reluctantly agreed to provide the men, to be ready the very next day. The following morning, once the miniature army had assembled, Oscar Jahnsen locked the hall's doors, divided the men into four groups, and briefed them on what lay ahead.

At Long Beach, Warren Olney and Deputy District Attorneys William Brayton and Russell Parsons would head up the *Tango* invasion, while Burdette Daniels of the attorney general's office would take charge of the raid on the *Mount Baker*. At Santa Monica—in view of George Contreras's predisposition to seasickness—Captain Walter Hunter, chief of the sheriff's vice squad, and Deputy District Attorney Clarence Hunt would lead the team that boarded the *Rex*. Contreras would be along, but below deck. Oscar Jahnsen would oversee the raid on the *Texas*.

At 3 P.M. that same day, Earl Warren, Warren Olney, and colleague Burdette Daniels departed Long Beach in Fish and Game Commission patrol boats with some fifty deputies, bound for the *Tango* and the *Mount Baker*. Behind each patrol boat trailed four of the taxis Olney had hired. Both Olney and Daniels had in hand copies of the original notice of abatement of a nuisance, and also a restraining order issued by Judge Wilson, felony warrants for bookmaking, and warrants for violation of the state penal code issued by Fitts.

To the relief of Daniels, the *Mount Baker's* operators offered little or no resistance. Once served with the orders and warrants, they promptly surrendered. All but ten of the surprised patrons were helped into taxis

and sent on their way to shore. Daniels arrested the unfortunate ten on charges of bookmaking, although the charges were later dismissed.

Warren Olney, on the other hand, ran into trouble with the *Tango*. There were no patrons aboard her, indicating that there had been a tip-off to what was coming. Specifically named in the restraining order against the *Tango* were her captain, Waldemar Vendshus, and presumed owners Clarence Blazier, A.C. Peters, and Donald Hull.

The *Tango*'s landing platform was equipped with an overhead steel door that could be cranked down to prevent access. As the raiding party approached, the door was already descending, shutting off the platform. A stern "No!" emanated from somewhere on the deck in response to Olney's request to board. He stayed calm. "O.K.," he yelled in return, "we'll come back later," and ordered the patrol boat's helmsman to head for the *Mount Baker* while he pondered what to do next.

The satisfactory status of the *Mount Baker* was heartening. Olney decided to return to the *Tango*, this time with fewer deputies and no taxis. Olney crowded as many deputies as possible into the hull of the Fish and Game patrol boat and, leaving his taxis tied to the *Mount Baker*, took off for another try.

This time, only he and the helmsman were visible to the *Tango*'s crew, who assumed, as Olney had hoped they would, that he had given up on invading and was returning simply to parley. Accordingly, they cranked up the steel door, exposing the landing platform. Olney waved his thanks, clambered onto the platform, and promptly positioned himself so that his shoulder was holding the door up by blocking access to the crankhole.

Instantly, the deputies in the patrol boat began piling onto the platform. The crew member holding the crank handle lunged at Olney, arm raised to strike him with it, but a deputy grabbed the upraised limb, pulled the handle from him, and tossed it into the sea. That was the extent of the violence. Heavily outnumbered by deputies, the *Tango* crew surrendered. The two accountants, who of course had also been squeezed into the patrol boat's hold, saw no sign of danger to and climbed hastily aboard. Following them into the ship's office, Olney saw an incredible amount of money—what looked like thousands of silver dollars.

Olney's next step was to assure the money aboard the *Tango* and the *Mount Baker*, was carefully counted, receipted, and transferred back to shore and to a bank for safekeeping. Olney had not anticipated, however, that most of the money consisted of heavy silver dollars. Taken together, the two ships were carrying some seventy-five thousand dollars in silver. Trying to bag that much bullion by hand and load it onto boats at night while pitching up and down on black waters would involve the unacceptable risk of accidental losses over the ships' sides. Leaving it in place, though, was an open invitation to hijacking (a primary concern of all the floating casinos). And the attorney general's men, having actually taken possession of the ships under summary abatement and disarmed their crews, were now responsible for their safekeeping.

# The Battle of Santa Monica Bay

Captain Walter Hunter, who was the chief of the sheriff's vice squad, and Deputy District Attorney Clarence Hunt sped their team to the *Rex*. Warren had greatly underestimated Cornero. The raid on the *Rex* became a drama recounted in local, national, and even international news for weeks. Tipped off to the impending raid, Cornero disarmed every crew member whose job entailed carrying a weapon. One shot from the *Rex*, he knew, would irreparably compromise the public's perception of an oppressor attorney general conducting a vendetta against a defenseless and law-abiding citizen's efforts to protect his legitimate business.

On that afternoon of August 1, as the armed contingent neared the *Rex*—the ship Earl Warren wanted most to knock out, and for whose operator his feelings bordered on contempt—the immense steel door of her landing platform slammed down, locking the raiders out and some six hundred patrons and two hundred employees in. To keep the approaching craft from coming any closer, *Rex* crewmen hauled out high-pressure hoses, took aim at the enemy, and sent powerful streams of water directly at them. Cornero appeared on deck and shouted his defiance using a megaphone:

> You cannot come on board this ship. We are beyond the three-mile limit. You're just a lousy bunch of pirates! We are on the high seas, and it's our own business whether we stay here one day or ten years. We are not defying any constitutional authority!

Near the *Rex* at this time was a U.S. Coast Guard cutter whose captain was mindful of the policy issued by Commander Bennett of the Guard's Southern California District:

> Coast Guard ships are to "observe" the stormy attempts to board the gambling ships. This is an unusual case, and what procedure we will take depends on the circumstances. Coast Guard men cannot demand that officers be allowed to board ships beyond the three-mile limit. However, we would not try to prevent them from boarding as they are trying to enforce the laws of the State. We will be in the area just in case any violence arises.

Cornero's relations with the Guard were good. Indeed, he had already notified the cutter that the stand

**Opposite:** On August 1, 1939, California Attorney General Earl Warren launched a raid on all four gambling ships, *Mount Baker* and *Tango* at Long Beach and *Rex* and *Texas* at Santa Monica. All but Cornero and his *Rex* surrendered immediately. His crew dissuaded the water taxis loaded with police from coming near the ship by using high-pressure water hoses to keep them away.

84
S.S. REX

NOIR AFLOAT

The Battle of Santa Monica Bay

85
S.S. REX

he was going to take against any invading party meant some six hundred afternoon patrons of the *Rex* would be aboard when the loading platform gate closed. Cornero was wary of being perceived by the police or the press as holding his passengers hostage. To this end, Cornero brokered a deal with the Coast Guard captain, Hunter, and Hunt whereby he would open the landing platform and allow the stranded patrons to be taxied by the police back to land. The raiding team, it was agreed, would not attempt to board the *Rex* in the process. All parties adhered to the deal, leaving only Tony and his seventy-five-man crew on the ship.

In that summer of 1939, the Santa Monica police station had been temporarily relocated to the La Monica Ballroom on the Santa Monica Pier while a new city hall was being constructed. Police Chief Dice turned the station into a temporary headquarters for Warren's operation. From 3 P.M. on, as news of the raids spread through Santa Monica and its environs, large crowds of spectators were gathering on Palisades Park hoping to get a glimpse of the action.

In addition, small craft of every type, many hired by reporters and photographers, chugged or sailed, minnow-like around and past the big Fish and Game boats, the Coast Guard cutters, and the floating casinos. Hunter and Hunt, unable to board the *Rex*, returned to shore. The attorney general ordered them to make a second attempt at dusk. This time, accepting the advice of those who had dealt with Tony Cornero in the past, he agreed that Sheriff's Captain Contreras would be in control of any communications with the *Rex*. Contreras knew Cornero, having dealt with him during Prohibition when Cornero was a rumrunner. Warren also ordered Fish and Game boats *Dolphin* and *Bonita*, both stocked with deputies, out to sea as well, with instructions to continue to circle the *Rex* throughout the night should the second try prove unsuccessful.

As the *Marlin* approached, Cornero and his crew stood ready with their high-pressure hoses. Wanting to avoid another barrage of water, the Fish and Game boat kept its distance from the *Rex*. Contreras, obviously suffering from motion sickness, saw his old acquaintance leaning over the rail of the *Rex* and, summoning up what strength he could, asked him if he would this time let the officers board to serve the restraining order. Once again, Cornero refused. At a complete impasse, Contreras's boat returned to shore, leaving the *Dolphin* and the *Bonita* to circle the *Rex* to be sure nobody left or boarded her.

Back on Santa Monica Pier, Attorney General Warren addressed the reporters hungry for an update:

> We've made good our promise to close up the gambling ships. If we don't arrest all the operators and the dealers and the others responsible for this appalling situation tonight, we'll get 'em tomorrow. Or we'll starve 'em out. We're prepared to besiege them until they give up.
>
> The banner of decency has been unfurled over these ships of chance. Although our men are not on board the *Rex*, we have the situation just as much under control there as in the case of the three other boats, because no one can board or leave the vessel. If Cornero seeks to avoid arrest, he either will have to stay on board indefinitely, or he will have to head straight out to sea. He can go as far as he likes in that direction!

The following day, the *Los Angeles Examiner* story on the raid put a different spin on the events:

*"You cannot come on board this ship. We are beyond the three-mile limit. You are just a lousy bunch of pirates! We are on the high seas and it's our own business whether we stay here one day or ten years. We are not defying any constitutional authority!"*

—TONY CORNERO

**Tony Cornero, at the rail of the *Rex* (third from right with overcoat and hat), yelled defiantly at the police.**

**The Battle of Santa Monica Bay**

87
S.S. REX

Like a mighty mariner of the days of wooden ships and iron men, the formidable Tony Cornero Stralla, a tough little guy, sent the law on its way yesterday and maintained the freedom of the seas for the gambling ship *Rex.*

As the night wore on, the weather turned cold and foggy and Cornero tossed bottles of his best scotch down to the tired deputies on the *Bonita* and the *Dolphin* circling the *Rex.* As the sun came up, the *Marlin* returned for a third time, this time carrying not only a weary Contreras and the deputies, but also Assistant Attorney General Paul McCormick and District Attorney Investigator John Klein. Again, Cornero steadfastly refused to surrender the *Rex.* Nor would he allow the officials to serve him with the documents they had in hand: Judge Wilson's restraining order and the district attorney's warrant for his arrest for violating the gambling statutes of the state penal code, and a new warrant for his arrest for "conspiracy to commit bookmaking."

To the delight of the numerous reporters who had tagged along behind the *Marlin,* Cornero came on deck and expounded on the law:

> Warren's Navy is nothing but a bunch of pirates. . . If we had shot them down, no court in the world would have held that they were justified in boarding a ship on the high seas. . . We're on the high seas. . . the state courts of California say so. . . Warren and Fitts are just look-ing for a political build-up. . . Warren, Fitts, the sheriff, and Superior Judge Emmett Wilson, who granted the injunction yesterday, are in my estimation, and verified by competent legal advice, in contempt of the State Supreme Court. . . The way I look at it, while this matter [ju-risdiction over the *Rex*] is before the Supreme Court, any action by law enforcement officers is in contempt of that Court! Moreover, there is enough food aboard to feed us all for a year.

From the beginning of his all-out crusade against the gambling ships, Attorney General Warren, sus-picious of the motives of the Los Angeles County district attorney and sheriff, correctly anticipated that they would be reluctant to go along with his drastic plan. He resorted to a political threat to bring them around. When that tactic succeeded, he was less than completely forthcoming about his overall intentions. Hamstrung by Tony Cornero, he wound up forcing Fitts, Biscailuz, and even himself into an increasingly embarrassing situation.

Day and night, the deputy-laden Fish and Game Commission boats of "Warren's Navy," as Tony in-sisted on loudly and publicly describing them, continued their circular stalking of the big *Rex,* tagged by nu-merous curious small craft, all under the watchful eye of one or another Coast Guard cutter. Neither Fitts nor Biscailuz were willing to brave the high-pressure hoses in an effort to board and take over the *Rex* by force. They remained unconvinced by the attorney general's insistence that the remedy of "summary abatement" under the nuisance statutes was applicable in situations involving more than one jurisdiction. Thus they felt committed

*Opposite:* **On August 10, 1939, Tony Cornero surrendered and stepped off the California Fish and Game boat onto the Santa Monica Pier, followed by Captain George Contreras.**

The Battle of Santa Monica Bay

89
S.S. REX

only to making sure the *Rex* stayed put and remained closed, and to serving her proprietor with the restraining order and warrants, but only when they could do so peaceably.

Accordingly, they left the next move up to the none-too-predictable Anthony Cornero Stralla.

To the growing amusement of the public, Cornero seemed in no hurry to act. But on the morning of August 10, 1939, having defied the enemy for ten long days, Tony appeared on deck, hailed the nearest press boat, and asked to be taken to the *Marlin*. Upon climbing aboard her, Cornero demanded: "Where's Contreras?" The veteran sheriff's captain, slightly seasick but jauntily clad in a white yachting outfit replete with a captain's hat and a colorful bandana around his neck, sauntered over, grinning, from the ship's cabin. "I understand," said Tony cheerfully, "that you have a warrant for my arrest." "Sure do," replied Contreras. "O.K.," rejoined Tony, "I surrender to you as a representative of the sheriff on that specific warrant, and I demand to be taken to the nearest magistrate." The warrant he referred to was that charging him with conspiracy to commit bookmaking. Cornero made it plain that he was surrendering only himself, not the *Rex*. She would remain at sea, carefully guarded by his seventy-five good and true crewmen, and with her high-pressure hoses primed. At Contreras's order, the *Marlin* sped shoreward. Reporters were waiting at the pier, of course, and their first question was a chorus: "Why did you give up, Tony?" "I surrendered," said the undaunted entrepreneur, "because I needed a haircut, and the only thing we don't have on the ship is a barber!"

Conveniently present at the pier to greet Tony were a bail bondsman and an attorney for the *Rex*, which did not surprise George Contreras in the least. Indeed, he assumed Tony had instructed both to meet him there that day. Over

**Tony Cornero and George Contreras discuss his surrender at the Santa Monica police headquarters on the Santa Monica Pier.**

Left: Oscar Jahnsen, chief investigator for the attorney general, served a search warrant to James Strange, chief engineer of the *Rex*, who was watching over the ship.
Right: Captain George Contreras and John Klein look at IOU slips on board the *Rex*.
Below: After Cornero surrendered, authorities boarded his ship.

the years, Cornero and the sheriff's captain seemed to have developed a kind of insight into each other, together with a certain mutual respect. Accordingly, Contreras served Tony the felony bookmaking warrant and the temporary restraining order he had been resisting. As Contreras had also anticipated, Tony accepted it without comment. Contreras had reasoned all along that although Tony would openly defy any official on earth whom he felt was unfairly attacking him, and would not want to be held in contempt of court by failing to appear before Judge Emmet Wilson on August 11. He had simply held out until the last possible moment—perhaps to give his lawyers maximum strategizing time, perhaps to utterly exasperate Earl Warren. Certainly it was obvious—despite of the attorney general's periodic public pronouncements to the contrary—that Anthony Cornero Stralla had succeeded admirably in that regard.

The nearest magistrate was located at the Santa Monica Police Court. After submitting to the usual mug shots, fingerprinting, and frisking at the Santa Monica police station, Tony presented himself before Santa Monica Municipal Judge Ellis Eagan. Explaining that he did not have authority to arraign under the particular circumstances, Judge Eagan released him on five thousand dollars bail and ordered him to appear for arraignment before Judge Wilbur Curtis in Los Angeles Municipal Court early the following morning.

As Contreras and Cornero shook hands before going their separate ways, the jovial free-on-bail proprietor of the *Rex* delivered a solemn warning to the exhausted sheriff's captain: "You guys," Tony said, "are violating the Constitution by maintaining a State Navy."

On August 25, 1939, Cornero appeared before Judge William McKay in Los Angeles Municipal Court to answer the felony bookmaking charge. Three days later, McKay dismissed the charges on grounds of lack of jurisdiction, citing the still-pending case before the California Supreme Court. An angry Attorney General Warren rushed to comment, but took no overt action. At the same time, an FBI agent reported to headquarters that Olney was concerned about an illegal wiretap on Cornero, ordered by the attorney general's office, and the havoc that would occur if it were revealed. No wonder it took decades for Olney to disclose publicly that Cornero had paid off McKay. Ironically, the moralistic Warren had backed himself into a corner. Because his wiretap broke state law, the state attorney general couldn't nail Cornero. Tony was free for the time being, but Warren was not finished with him.

On November 20, 1939, the California Supreme Court addressed the question of whether the waters off Santa Monica constituted a bay. The Court ruled that all the waters known as Santa Monica Bay indeed conformed to the definition of a bay, were within the territorial waters of the State of California, and were therefore within that state's jurisdiction. The Court noted that the waters had been known as a bay for at least four hundred years, during a large portion of which they had been used as a harbor. It specifically stated that the jurisdiction of the state over the waters of the bay in question extended landward from a line drawn between its headlands—Point Vicente and Point Dume—and oceanward from that line for a distance of at least three miles. Such jurisdiction could be exercised by the state for all proper purposes, including prosecution of violators of the state penal code. The phrase "at least" before "three miles" was actually inserted in response to the attorney general pointing out that the wording of the decision ought not to have the effect of precluding the state from claiming jurisdiction over the waters surrounding California's offshore islands.

To be outside state jurisdiction, therefore, a ship would have to be over fifteen miles from the Santa Monica shoreline. Cornero's insistence that the waters were a "bight" and not a "bay" had been soundly rejected at the highest level.

Cornero announced that the Supreme Court's decision had rendered his position untenable, and thus he would surrender. Accompanied by his attorney Jerry Geisler, he arrived at Attorney General Warren's office in San Francisco to negotiate his surrender. Warren allowed Geisler into his office, but not Cornero. Perhaps because of his knowledge of Geisler's skills at litigation, Warren opened the meeting by threatening that if Cornero continued to appeal the cases pending against him, he would see to it that Cornero was charged with pay-

ing off Judge McKay for the favorable decision in his bookmaking case. Warren asserted that he had proof of the payoff, but did not reveal that the proof he alluded to had been obtained through an illegal wiretap of Cornero's phone. Geisler, who had defended Tony in that case, pleasantly replied that if Warren's charge were proved, his own ego would be severely bruised, inasmuch as he had been sure his own legal ability had been responsible for Tony's victory. He then politely asked permission to leave the room to consult briefly with his client.

When he returned minutes later, Geisler made no reference to the threat regarding McKay, and simply informed Earl Warren that Cornero was willing to "end the whole thing on whatever terms the attorney general thought fair," although he had given Geisler permission, as his attorney, to point out anything that might seem inadvertently unjust.

The final settlement negotiated required Cornero to abandon his appeal of the permanent injunction against operation of the *Rex*, and any other gambling ship now or in the future, to allow the state to destroy the *Rex*'s gambling paraphernalia, to pay $4,200 in property taxes, to produce all books and other missing records of the *Rex* for computation of state income taxes for the years 1938 and 1939, and to pay such taxes. Additionally, Cornero would be required to pay $7,500 in settlement of the State Railroad Commission's $496,000 suit against him and his associates for failure to obtain licenses and post tariffs and fees for water taxis plying between Santa Monica and the *Rex*, and to pay $13,200 in abatement costs to reimburse the attorney general's office for expenses incurred in attempts to board the *Rex* and the ensuing blockade. In exchange, the attorney general agreed to return to Cornero the money confiscated from the *Rex*—the ship's bankroll.

On November 21, 1939, two Fish and Game Commission boats, the *Tuna* and the *Broadbill*, brought Jahnsen and Deputy Attorney General Paul McCormick, the sheriff's captains George Contreras and Walter Hunter, District Attorney Chief Investigator John Klein, and a score of deputies once again, out to the *Rex* still anchored off Santa Monica. The *Broadbill* also carried members of the press, including photographers. Prepared to be soaked by high-pressure hoses and barred from boarding, the officials were unaware that Cornero had already reached his settlement with Warren and had phoned the *Rex* to tell the crew to offer no resistance.

Upon boarding, James Strange, chief engineer of the *Rex*, came up on deck and accepted the search warrant. Without commenting, he indicated that the only people aboard the *Rex* since her closing had been himself, to keep an eye on the power plant, and his assistant, Victor Simian, to maintain the radiotelephone.

Jahnsen began the search in the main salon. The gambling equipment appeared to have been left in place, but all of it was covered with thick dust and cloths thrown carelessly over the gaming tables. During the search, a small craft pulled alongside and Warren Olney came aboard. When he arrived, the officials fanned out on a systematic and thorough search of the vessel. After the search, Olney gave the order to destroy the gambling paraphernalia.

The group heaved at least seventy slot machines overboard. Buckets of poker chips followed. Tossed high in the air, the chips rained down on the sea's surface, coloring the waves as they hit them, then slowly sinking. Using the ship's fire axes, the deputies splintered roulette wheels and hacked craps tables to pieces. Over $100,000 worth of the finest gambling equipment was reduced to useless scrap. Much of the wooden equip-

94
S.S. REX

Authorities toss slot machines, chips, and other gambling equipment into the ocean. Other officers took slot machines on small boats and scattered the machines into the sea.

The Battle of Santa Monica Bay

95
S.S. REX

Roulette wheels and tables were taken to the city dump, doused with kerosene, and set afire.
*Opposite:* Walter Hunt and Oscar Jahnsen (left), wet from tossing slot machines into the sea, pose for a photo, pretending to destroy a roulette wheel with a *Rex* fire axe.

ment, though chopped to pieces, became flotsam. The chunks were loaded into scows and hauled back to shore. The remains ultimately ended up in the Santa Monica dump, where they were set afire.

According to the settlement, the *Rex* was to remain Cornero's property. However, the ship was ultimately confiscated by the Alcohol Tax Unit to cover some of the taxes Cornero owed. The *Rex* was sold to Frank Hellenthal and Associates. Her new owners stripped her of everything, leaving only her hull. She was transformed into a six-masted schooner, renamed *Star of Scotland*, and put to work hauling lumber to South Africa. On November 13, 1942 while sailing from Cape Town to Paranagua, Brazil, a surfaced German U-59 submarine sank the fifty-five-year-old vessel by shell fire.

As the ship went down, her glamour days were half a decade and half a world away. But Tony Cornero was still in the game.

# Relentless

California Attorney General Earl Warren's successful campaign against the floating casinos, culminating in his 1939 raid of the *Texas*, the *Mount Baker*, the *Tango*, and the *Rex*, put an end to offshore gambling in California. A number of the gambling ship operators turned their eyes and fortunes to Nevada, where they invested in casinos in Las Vegas.

　　Tony Cornero went to Havana, Cuba, where he took over a casino called Montmartre Club. After he turned it into a successful operation, the chief of police wanted the casino for himself. He persuaded his boss, dictator Fulgencio Batista, to kick Cornero and his partner Fred Grange out of Cuba.

NOIR AFLOAT

S. S. REX

**LOOK**

# S. S. REX

## NOW ANCHORED IN LAS VEGAS
APACHE HOTEL BLDG. — Corner Second and Fremont

★

*Grand Opening*

## TOMORROW NIGHT
SATURDAY, MARCH 3

★ CRAPS     ★ ROULETTE
★ PAN       ★ RACE HORSE KENO
★ FARO      ★ RACE BOOK
★ POKER     ★ TWENTY-ONE

*Rex Club*

2ND and FREMONT
LAS VEGAS, NEV.

CLOSE COVER BEFORE STRIKING

From there Tony went to Las Vegas and for a short time was a partner in a casino on Fremont Street called the S.S. Rex Club. Trouble started with the Nevada Gaming Commission when partners were caught carrying loaded weapons in the casino. The commission stated they would not renew the license if Cornero and others remained as partners. At that, Cornero ended his partnership.

**The S.S. Rex Club, named in honor of Cornero's great gambling ship, opened on Fremont Street in Las Vegas on March 2, 1945. It was located in the old Hotel Apache owned by P.O. Silvagni.**
*Opposite:* **An advertisement and chips are some of the last remnants of the short-lived Tony Cornero era in Havana, where he started a new life after the *Rex* was shut down.**

**Relentless**

## Bunker Hill/Lux

Cornero's next venture was a legitimate shipping business called the Seven Seas Trading Company. He purchased three ships to haul products between ports along the Pacific coast and as far away as Hong Kong.

On April 3, 1946, Cornero stunned the public with an announcement he would once again open gambling ships off the coast of California.

Earl Warren, who had been elected governor of California in 1943, assured the public that gambling ships would not operate off the California coast as long as he was in office.

Republican Senator William F. Knowland, perhaps less confident in California's ability to stop the likes of Cornero, stated that if state laws were not adequate to prevent offshore gambling, it will be the responsibility of the federal government to pass appropriate legislation. And Los Angeles Mayor Fletcher Bowron pledged that if any gambling boats dared to operate off the coast of his city, "somebody will go to jail."

Tony Cornero apparently wasn't the least bit concerned with what the authorities had to say. He said he planned to operate more than one gambling ship and that he already had them. Tony confidently boasted, "This time I will be perfectly safe. I've made sure of that. There'll be no way they can stop me from operating because everything I do will be perfectly legal. It will be several months before I get these ships into operation. I plan to operate off the coast of Malibu."

Cornero purchased the *Bunker Hill* to be the first of his gambling fleet. The *Bunker Hill* was built to be a freighter in 1907. In 1911, she went to work for the Maine Steamship Company as a passenger ship, carrying passengers on the Boston-New York route. The next chapter in her storied career was as a minelayer for the U.S. Navy during World War I. For this incarnation she was renamed the

**A picture postcard showcases the steamship *Bunker Hill* when she worked for the Eastern Steamship Corporation from 1912 to 1917.**

*Aroostook* and helped lay the North Sea Mine Barrage intended to destroy German submarines. Then she was converted by the navy into an aircraft tender. The navy decommissioned her in 1931, and she remained idle for twelve years. On February 5, 1943, she went to the Maritime Commission for use as a World War II barracks ship for the U.S. Army. When the war ended, the *Aroostook* went to the Dulien Steel Products Company in Seattle to be scrapped, but was saved when Cornero purchased her.

After a week in tow from Seattle to Long Beach, the ex-*Aroostook* arrived looking like a broken-down rusty derelict. At this point, Cornero's vessel was officially nameless—when the U.S. Navy sells a ship they sell only the vessel, not its name. Tied to a bulkhead near the east end of the Cerritos Channel in the harbor, workers began the transformation of the rusty hulk into a luxurious gambling casino.

Cornero announced he would call his gambling ship *Luxurious*. Newspapers dubbed her *Lux* for short, and the name stuck. From then on Cornero referred to his ship as the S.S. *Lux*. Cornero sold the S.S. *Lux* to the Sevenseas Trading and Steamship Company, the Nevada corporation he had established for his legitimate shipping company, and of which he was president. He sold shares in the enterprise, in five-thousand-dollar increments. No receipts or written records of the transactions were provided to investors. Business with Cornero, at least in the arena of gambling ships, was strictly verbal and based on trust. Gamblers and investors who knew Cornero said they considered him an honest and shrewd businessman.

FBI records reveal that Wilbur Clark, formerly associated with the Las Vegas gambling casino El Rancho, became one of the major investors in Cornero's enterprise. Clark was a longtime friend of Cornero. He started his career as a gambler in San Diego, and was later a craps dealer on the gambling ships *Johanna Smith* and *Tango*. He also worked as a

The rusty hull of the ex-mine layer *Aroostook*, ex-*Bunker Hill*, ties up at Long Beach. She was converted into a gambling ship called *Lux* by Tony Cornero in 1946.

dealer for Cornero on the *Rex*. He achieved wealth and notoriety through his association with the El Rancho and later the Desert Inn in Las Vegas. Cornero did not describe Clark as a principal investor, but rather one of fifty associates in the Sevenseas Trading and Steamship Company. He described the company as a fifty-member co-partnership composed of Southern California business people. He denied claims that "Las Vegas money" was supporting his new enterprise, preferring to say it was privately financed. According to FBI records, Clark had more than a million dollars deposited in the Sevenseas bank account. It was estimated he had more than a hundred thousand dollars of his own money invested in the *Lux*. He also acted as Cornero's Las Vegas intermediary. Gamblers in Las Vegas would approach him and say, "Here's five thousand, cut me in on Tony's deal." Clark took the money and gave it to Cornero.

At the time Cornero was working on his gambling ship in Long Beach, Benjamin "Bugsy" Siegel was trying to finish construction of his Flamingo Hotel on the Strip in Las Vegas. Siegel claimed he once had a partnership in Cornero's *Rex*, but pulled out after a disagreement. The two men purportedly disliked each other, and at this time Siegel surely did not want competition from him.

After the closure of the gambling ships in 1939, the California legislature took no steps to prevent a

**This photograph captures the starboard side of the completed *Lux*/*Bunker Hill*, and both names are clearly visible on the stern and hull of the ship, as it anchors off Long Beach, ready for business.**

NOIR AFLOAT

recurrence. Coastal towns did not bother to remove or to change the ineffective and unconstitutional ordinances from their books. The federal government still lacked laws to prevent gambling ships from operating in federal waters. To remedy this, Republican Senator William Knowland of California introduced Bill SB 2199. The proposed bill would render the operation of a gambling ship within the admiralty and maritime jurisdiction of the United States and outside the jurisdiction of any particular state a federal offense. Violations would be punishable by fines up to $10,000 and imprisonment of not more than two years. The bill would also make it illegal to transport people to gambling ships. Senator Knowland presented the bill near the end of the 1939 congressional session. He spoke before the Senate Judiciary Committee, headed by Senator Pat McCarran, a Democrat from Nevada, urging the committee to approve the bill with a favorable report to the Senate. It was no secret Senator McCarran watched over the interests of the gamblers in his home state of Nevada, and he did not hide his lack of enthusiasm for the legislation. He told Senator Knowland he wanted to wait until he received input from Attorney General Tom C. Clark about the pending bill. During this process of further study, the bill died on the Senate calendar.

Upon completion, the *Lux* was painted all white. Electricians placed three red neon tubes, one above the other, surrounding the top deck. The brilliant red light would be visible from the shore both day and night.

A major hurdle for Cornero concerned the documentation and registration of his vessel. The U.S. Coast Guard was determined to make Cornero follow all rules and regulations to the letter. It would not issue a certificate of inspection unless he documented the ship. Cornero hoped to avoid this. The Coast Guard said, "No documentation, no certificate." A certificate of inspection shows that a ship has been found seaworthy, states the number of passengers and crew allowed on board, and lists the name of the captain or master. Coast Guard regulations require its display in a prominent place. The certificate was critical if Cornero expected to take his ship out to sea, since no vessel can legally sail without one. The Coast Guard and Customs Office at San Pedro had discussed the documentation issue, and decided that the certificate would be issued unless Cornero documented his ship.

When Cornero learned the original name of his ship was *Bunker Hill*, he thought the name should stay with the vessel because he didn't believe in changing vessels' original names. On August 5, 1946, he gave in and documented his ship with the name *Bunker Hill*, and listed Los Angeles as her home port. For registry purposes he had four classification choices: fishing, whaling, foreign trade, or coastwise trade. Cornero, it would later turn out, made his most critical mistake in this venture when he chose the category of coastwise trade. Following regulations, painters painted the name *Bunker Hill* on the bow on both the port and starboard sides. On the stern, were the words *Bunker Hill* and Los Angeles, her home port. In a move not called for in any government or maritime regulation, Tony also instructed painters to put the word *LUX* in four-foot-high letters in two places

**Gambling tables and games were set up for the anticipated crowds that would soon storm aboard on opening night. The vast interior was ready for thousands of players and onlookers.**

NOIR AFLOAT

on the starboard side of the vessel. Cornero had already opened a bank account under that name. He had also ordered stationery, checks, and other printed matter with S.S. Lux printed on them. Gambling chips, dice and menus were also imprinted with the name. For these reasons Cornero felt justified in painting *LUX* on his ship as well. Upon her completion, the impressive *Lux* was towed to a spot 7.3 miles southeast of the Los Angeles harbor lighthouse, at least a mile beyond County waters, and anchored five and one-half miles due south of the Naples section of Long Beach, which is 2.75 miles south of the Orange County line. Long Beach and Orange County authorities did not have the power or legal means to stop Cornero.

California Attorney General Robert W. Kenny's office checked liquor distributors and found no liquor

**Opening night on the *Lux* was a success. The vessel's capacity under the law was 2,038, but the crowd was more than three thousand.**

went from Los Angeles County to the *Lux*. Kenny's office also checked with the Los Angeles and Orange County offices of the Board of Equalization to see if anyone filed an application for a liquor license on behalf of Cornero. They found none. Cornero did not apply for a license because by his reckoning he would not be selling liquor in California.

Once again, the exact location of California's three-mile limit still challenged and confused authorities. Before Cornero opened the S.S. *Lux*, California Attorney General Kenny said that he believed California's three-mile limit extended beyond all the Channel Islands, stretching from the Santa Barbara Islands through San Clemente and Santa Catalina Islands. Kenny declared, "My office will arrest Cornero the minute he operates, unless he is three miles beyond the western shore of Catalina. Although gambling is legal on the high seas, it is ridiculous to think that high seas separate parts of the same country." He was seeking legal support for his theory so he could prosecute Cornero under California's anti-gambling statutes. If Kenny was correct, California's three-mile limit would be at least thirty-five miles from shore. A variety of other court decisions added to the confusion. One held that San Pedro Bay was all the water inside a line drawn from Point Fermin to Newport Beach. Another held that San Pedro Bay was the area within a line drawn from Point Fermin to Huntington Beach. Arguments were rampant. No one, it seemed, knew for sure exactly how far California's legal jurisdiction reached out to sea.

Originally, it had been the responsibility of Los Angeles County District Attorney Fred N. Howser to stop Cornero when the *Lux* was under construction in San Pedro. State officials criticized Howser for his lack of action. Howser claimed he didn't know how to stop Cornero. Former District Attorney Warren Olney reminded Howser that Cornero had accepted a permanent injunction in 1939. This injunction applied not only to the *Rex*, but to any future gambling ship. Howser would have only needed to issue a citation to Cornero to appear in court and show cause why he shouldn't be punished for violating the injunction. But Howser did nothing.

California Attorney General Kenny believed that Cornero may have bribed Howser. His suspicions were confirmed in an office memorandum dated August 29, 1946, to J. Edgar Hoover, director of the FBI. In it, the agent reported that Tony Cornero and his associates offered Fred Howser twenty-five thousand dollars to permit them to operate the ship without interference. Howser countered with thirty-five thousand dollars, and they struck a deal. Howser was cornered. To give the appearance he was trying to stop Tony, he said he would allow the ship to operate for twenty-four hours, long enough for him to gather legal evidence that gambling was going on, then he would clamp down.

The *Lux* opened for business on the evening of August 6. Throughout the night water taxis brought more than three thousand people from the Long Beach dock of the offshore water taxi company to the ship. The gambling room on the main deck was 420 feet long and 52 feet wide. Located down the center of the deck were twelve roulette wheels, fourteen craps tables, twelve blackjack tables, five poker tables, two chuck-a-luck games, and other gambling devices. In the racetrack section, one could bet on any race on any track in the country with track odds. Along one side of the room and spread the length of the ship were 129 slot machines, set to receive coins from five cents to a dollar. Of that number, thirty Pace Deluxe Bell slot machines belonged to the

**One hundred twenty-nine Jennings Bronze Chief slot machines lined the walls of the *Lux*.**

Automatic Games Company, who paid seventy percent of the machines' profits to the ship. Cornero owned the remainder of the slots, which were Jennings Bronze Chief machines. On the opposite wall stood a bar 110 feet long displaying rare and imported scotches and Champagnes. The forward end of the main deck was a bingo parlor with space for a hundred players. This concession was rented to William Berkley, who paid one hundred dollars per day for the privilege of operating on the ship.

Many people came with no intention of gambling, but only to see the ship and enjoy people-watching, or to dine and dance. The small dance floor was about seven by nine feet, accommodating only a few couples at a time. The orchestra played for only six days. The musicians' union demanded a contract and Cornero refused to sign one. As a result, the union would not allow musicians to play on the ship thereafter. On the upper deck stood a nightclub with a liquor bar thirty feet long, and a restaurant with accommodations for three hundred guests. The upper deck was large enough for three or four hundred people to stroll or simply enjoy the sea air.

After two days of profitable operation, with capacity crowds already on board and hundreds of gamblers anxiously waiting in line at the dock, Long Beach authorities made their move. On August 8 at about 6:30 in the evening, thirty police officers arrived at the dock of the water taxi company. Two officers climbed aboard each craft. Once headed out to sea, they warned each water taxi operator that his next trip would violate the Long Beach ordinance prohibiting passage to gambling ships. Police allowed the taxis to make the trip to the *Lux* and discharge their passengers; upon returning to the dock they arrested the operators and impounded the taxis. Police arrested twenty pilots and dockhands. Long Beach police kept the impounded water taxis, ten in all, under surveillance. Customers waiting on the dock for their rides to the ship hurled catcalls and obscenities at the authorities and stood their ground. Nobody made a move to leave. Cars backed up, bumper to bumper for three

The *Lux* operated for two days before the authorities raided and closed the ship, accusing Cornero of violating the terms of his license. Anxious passengers pushed and shoved to get a spot on a water taxi heading for shore. Some customers who were stranded on the *Lux* overnight slept any place they could find, including the bingo parlor.

NOIR AFLOAT

It required two powerful tugs, the *Louie Black* and the *Crowley No. 29*, to tow the *Lux* back into the harbor. The marooned passengers were still on board the gambling ship.

blocks, stopping traffic.

The arrest of the water taxi operators marooned a thousand people on board the ship overnight. Since the ship offered little or no accommodations for sleeping, lounging, or sitting, patrons had to wander around aimlessly or sleep on top of the gaming tables or on the floor. The water taxis finally arrived the next day to remove the stranded patrons. By this time many were angry, suffering from fatigue, seasickness, and extreme nervousness. There is no doubt that some were thinking up good excuses to tell the wife where they had been all night.

The Orange County coastal communities of Newport Beach, Seal Beach, and Huntington Beach prepared ordinances to block water taxis operating from their towns. Los Angeles Mayor Fletcher Bowron said that any water taxis trying to operate from the Los Angeles harbor could expect immediate arrest.

On August 29, Judge Fred Miller directed that the water taxis impounded by the district attorney be returned to their owner, George Garvin. Garvin insisted he had no connection with Cornero or the ship. Two days later Garvin's taxis were once again taking passengers to the *Lux*.

In a move to protect themselves, the water taxi company erected a large sign on the pier informing patrons that:

The owners, operators, and crews of the water taxis do not solicit anyone to visit any particular destination. The operators do not have any connection with any ship, business, or other enterprise.

After the water taxi put to sea, the operator then asked his passengers for their destination. If they replied the gambling ship, they collected a fifty-cent fare without comment. If a passenger should jokingly say Catalina Island or any other destination, the operator promptly said the fare would be fifty dollars, but that the taxi would need to make one stop first.

Long Beach Chief of Police Alvin Slaight and his officers made more than fifty arrests. Still the water taxis continued to operate.

Howser then arrested Tony Cornero, Elmer Perry, Ernie Judd, Frank A. Gruber, George Garvin (water taxi operator), and Robert Menzies (the ship's captain), and charged them with conspiring to violate state gambling laws. They were released after each paid a two-thousand-dollar bond.

On September 7, many thought labor union pickets would do what law enforcement officers were unable to do: close Tony Cornero's gambling ship. The Master Mates and Pilots Association Local No. 90 A.F.L. formed a picket line at the water taxi landing, protesting Cornero's refusal to employ a first, second, and third mate on the ship. The Sailors' Union of the Pacific also reestablished its picket line at the parking lot entrance after negotiations broke down to put eighteen certified seamen-lifeboat men aboard the vessel. Captains of the picket lines said they were there not only there to keep the water taxi operators from operating their boats to and from the *Lux*, but to keep union members from visiting the ship. For the next ten days, the gambling ship remained open and filled to capacity with patrons who chose to ignore the union picket line.

On September 17, 1946, the federal government made its move. United States Attorney General Tom C. Clark ordered the seizure of the *Bunker Hill*, claiming that the ship violated the terms of her license. She was licensed for coastwise trade, but was being utilized for another purpose—illegal gambling. Federal authorities noted the *Bunker Hill* had been standing still since the day she left the harbor and did not sail coastal waters or trade anything. In rebuttal, Cornero insisted that his ship *was* moving. He reasoned that since the ocean currents passed under the ship, she was never over the same water all the time, and therefore she must be moving. He also claimed he was involved with coastwise trade because the water taxis were taking customers on and off his ship.

United States Attorney James M. Carter filed the libel action to obtain forfeiture of the ship to the government. Two Coast Guard cutters, the *Hermes* and the *Yankton*, pulled up alongside the *Lux*. Commander Chester Anderson and armed Coast Guardsmen went aboard and announced that the United States had seized the ship.

Fifteen uniformed customs inspectors took charge of the ship. They placed seals on safes, cash registers, liquor vaults, and anything else of value they could find. The value of the ship's huge liquor stock and safe with its cash content together exceeded one hundred thousand dollars. Federal agents took fifty thousand silver dollars ashore and deposited them in a bank for safekeeping. Three hundred cases of unopened liquor went to

NOIR AFLOAT

After authorities emptied coins from the slot machines, filling thirty-four large moneybags with about fifteen thousand dollars in silver, the machines from the *Lux* were loaded on a barge, taken out to sea, and dumped into the ocean.

**Relentless**

a bonded warehouse. Agents emptied every slot machine and the coins filled thirty-four large moneybags with about fifteen thousand dollars in silver. These, too, went to the bank. Three custodians from the United States Marshal's office guarded the vessel while the government's libel action went through the courts.

The libel proceedings, brought under maritime and admiralty statutes, charged that:

1. The *Bunker Hill*, one-time navy minelayer, was licensed for coastwise trade and "no other employment," but actually was used exclusively for "commercial gambling."
2. The ship was duly documented as the S.S. *Bunker Hill*, but, by device, advertisement, and contrivance, the owners attempted to deceive the public and any officer of the United States . . . by calling her S.S. *Lux*.

On November 22, 1946, Federal Court Judge J.F.T. O'Conner ruled the *Bunker Hill* be forfeited to the government because it engaged in a business for which it was not licensed, finding that the ship "violated provisions of Revised Statutes 4377 (46 U.S.C. 325) and 4179 (46 U.S.C. 50) and acts amendatory thereto."

On December 13, 1946, Superior Judge William R. McKay found Cornero, George Garvin, Elmer Perry, and Ernie Judd not guilty of charges that they conspired to violate the California law that prohibited the solicitation of patronage for gambling establishments. Judge McKay issued a seventy-six-page written opinion explaining his findings. In it he reviewed previous gambling ship litigation, discussed that Nevada advertises for patrons in California, and concluded that California had no effective laws to prohibit the operation of gambling ships on the high seas off the coast. He also ruled that prosecutors had produced no evidence showing that the defendants or their employees had solicited patronage for their gambling ship. Judge McKay said during the trial that California's gambling laws were a mess. He wrote, "For instance, draw poker is legal throughout the state, and pari-mutuel betting is legal at authorized racetracks. . . I could go to a draw poker parlor and lose ten thousand dollars there without anybody violating any law. Yet, if I asked a friend to go along with me, just to watch, I would, under one legal interpretation, be guilty of a serious crime. The same situation applies at the racetracks, and it is most confusing."

Superior Judge William McKay, it should be noted, was the same judge who, as a municipal judge in 1939, dismissed a bookmaking charge against Cornero. It was commonly known at the time that he was paid by Cornero for that dismissal.

On January 8, 1947, Judge O'Conner ordered the confiscated vessel be turned over to the U.S. Treasury Department. At the same time, he ordered U.S. Marshal Bob Clark to destroy all gambling equipment on the floating casino. In addition, he instructed Clark to turn into the federal clerk's office the $36,000 in cash seized during the raid. The federal clerk had to withhold enough money to pay for court costs and maintenance on the ship. The remainder of the cash went to the Internal Revenue Service to satisfy any federal taxes.

The government stripped the *Bunker Hill* of virtually everything of value. The Treasury Department took possession of 487 cases of liquor. On February 19, 1947, federal agents poured a thousand bottles of partially emptied liquor confiscated from the ship's bar into the ocean. They hurled twenty thousand dollars' worth of Cornero's gambling equipment—consisting of 129 slot machines, three hundred thousand poker chips, eight cases of dice (fifty pair per case), two lottery cages and one chuck-a-luck cage—into three hundred fathoms of water five miles off of Point Fermin.

At the same time on shore, twelve roulette tables and wheels, forty dice and blackjack tables, two hundred dozen playing cards and miscellaneous items consisting of lottery cards, race horse betting sheets, etc., and other wooden gambling equipment were stacked in a pile, doused with gasoline and ignited.

Initially the *Lux* was to be towed to the U.S. Coast Guard Station in San Francisco to be placed in what they called "Death Row," a holding dock for derelict vessels to be towed out to sea and used for gunnery practice. The Coast Guard changed its mind, however, and the vessel went to Suisun Bay, where the Maritime Commission took her over. They put the ship up for sale for scrap, requesting sealed bids. In order to prevent Cornero from buying his ship back, the FBI intervened at this point and asked the Maritime Commission to furnish it the names of bidders.

On October 17, 1947, the Commission sold the *Lux* to the Basalt Rock Company, Inc. of Napa, which had submitted the highest bid: $18,000. The agreement stated the buyer had to dismantle and scrap the vessel within one year. Two months later, the Basalt Rock Company reported that the only remnant of the vessel still in existence was a center portion of the hull, which would be completely cut up during the next several days. The short but exciting life of the gambling ship *Bunker Hill* or *Lux* came to an unceremonious end, and brought to a close the saga of offshore gambling ships in California.

## Cornero Shot!

On February 10, 1948, at Tony Cornero's home at 312 South Elm Drive, in Beverly Hills, Tony and two men from Mexico sat in his living room having a serious conversation involving gambling casinos in Mexico. The doorbell rang, Tony opened the door to see a man holding a package. What he didn't see was the gun under the package. The man said, "We've got something for you, Tony!" He pulled the trigger, the gun barked, and one bullet tore into Cornero's stomach. The force of the gunshot caused Tony to stagger back and collapse on the floor.

An ambulance rushed Tony to Cedars of Lebanon Hospital, where doctors performed a two and one-half hour operation. The doctors said the bullet entered his abdomen and ripped out the terminal portion of the small intestine. Surgeons repaired that damage, but left the bullet that remained lodged near the spine to await a second operation. Tony remained in critical condition for nearly two weeks. Beverly Hills police investigators were at a loss. To find the would-be assassin, they needed clues. If Cornero knew who fired the shot, he would not admit it. When police questioned Tony, all he would say was, "I never seen the man before, and I don't have an enemy in the world who would want to shoot me." Since Cornero had been meeting with two Mexican officials to discuss opening gambling casinos in Mexico, Beverly Hills police theorized that a competing Mexican group bidding for gambling concessions shot Cornero to eliminate the competition. Others suggested it was a holdup attempt, and one even said it could have been a nervous prowler. Some speculated Tony had been shot in retaliation for the failure of the gambling ship *Bunker Hill/Lux*. If it had been a mob shooting, Tony would be dead—mobsters did not wound their victims; they killed them.

Cornero slowly recovered and regained his old energy. When he was well enough to travel, Chief of Police Clifford H. Anderson suggested he move out of Beverly Hills, supposedly to a safer spot. Anderson wasn't particularly concerned with Tony's well-being, but cared about the reputation of Beverly Hills and did not want to contend with any more gangland killings or shootings. Cornero's case and mobster Benjamin "Bugsy" Siegel's murder were untidy, unsolved crimes in the files of the Beverly Hills Police Department. The chief recommended that Tony move to Las Vegas.

Las Vegas was experiencing a spectacular development boom outside the city limits on the highway leading to Los Angeles, a road that was filled with huge hotels and casinos and which became known as the Las Vegas Strip. Cornero, fully aware of its importance, wanted a casino on the Strip. In 1954 he bought thirty-two acres of desert land located north of the bankrupt Hotel Nevada for $650,000, and planned to build the Stardust, the world's largest resort hotel and gambling casino. He formed a company called Stardust, Inc., then sold four million dollars of stock without bothering to register it with the Securities and Exchange Commission. To make matters worse, Cornero gambled and started to lose large chunks of the investors' money in casinos all over town. Before construction of the 1032-room hotel and casino reached the halfway mark, Cornero applied for his gaming license, which the Nevada Tax Commission refused to issue because of his troubles with the SEC. Knowing he would not get a license, Cornero leased the casino portion of the Stardust to eight men for six million dollars a year, retaining his position as president and general manager of the hotel. Milton B. "Farmer" Page, Tony's friend and past partner on the *Tango* and *Rex*, assumed Cornero's one-sixth interest in the casino. The tax commissioner approved the eight men for the gaming license, even though state officials knew they were a front for Cornero.

Tony never saw the completion of his dream hotel and casino. On July 31, 1955 at 10:40 in the morning, while shooting craps at the Desert Inn across the street from his nearly completed Stardust Hotel, he dropped dead from a heart attack. He was fifty-five years old.

Confusion, speculation, and deliberate misinformation caused intrigue surrounding Cornero's death. The *Las Vegas Review-Journal* reported that Tony had suffered from heart trouble for the past several years, and that he was stricken while standing at the dice table and then rushed to his room, where he died. The following day the *Las Vegas Review-Journal* reported several unusual circumstances regarding Tony's untimely death. Tony's personal physician, Dr. Alfred Ehrlich, contradicted the newspaper report by stating, "He was dead before he hit the floor." Tony's death certificate listed the cause of death as coronary thrombosis. It also stated that no autopsy was performed. In fact, the coroner was not notified until three hours after Cornero succumbed. Instead, a call was placed to the Edwards Brothers Mortuary in Los Angeles to remove Cornero's body. The mortuary then contacted Las Vegas coroner's officials and insisted they not touch Cornero's body; rather, Edwards Brothers would come to Las Vegas and take it directly to Los Angeles for embalming and burial.

Cornero poses in front of the Stardust, the hotel and casino he was building in Las Vegas. Before the casino was completed, he dropped dead, supposedly from a heart attack at the craps table of the Desert Inn, across the street from his last gambling venture. The Stardust opened July 2,1958, three years after Cornero's untimely death.

Rumors prevailed. Cornero's girlfriend said she was with him at the time of his death and insisted he did not die from a heart attack, but that he was murdered. She said somebody injected him with an undetectable lethal substance while he was in the men's room, that his assailants slumped him over the dice table, and called the doctor. Others guessed there was no way the eight men wanted to pay Cornero six million dollars a year, so they eliminated him.

It was a grand funeral at the Edwards Brothers Colonial Mortuary in Los Angeles. An overflow crowd of family and friends, including almost every hoodlum, gambler, and gangster in the country, attended the service. More than five hundred people crowded into the small chapel, anteroom, and gallery, and then spilled out into the street. The police dressed in plain clothes, mingled with the crowd, took photographs and motion pictures of those present, and worked feverishly to copy down the license plate numbers of the expensive cars driven by the mourners. The service lasted all of eight minutes.

On the front page of the *Las Vegas Review-Journal* a large headline proclaimed "Tony Rides to Heaven on Wabash Cannonball." The paper reported that western singer Dick Foote, who was scheduled for the opening show at the Stardust, sang Cornero's favorite song, adapting it a bit for Tony:

> *Here's to our pal, Tony, may his name forever stand.*
> *May it always be respected by his friends throughout the land.*
> *His earthly race is over and the curtain round him falls.*
> *He'll be carried up to heaven on the Wabash Cannonball.*

A procession of more than a hundred cars followed the hearse to Inglewood Park Cemetery, where Tony was laid to rest. The bodies of Tony, Frank, and their mother, Maddalena, now rest side by side in crypts at the Mausoleum of the Golden West.

The Stardust Hotel finally opened on July 2, 1958, almost three years after Cornero's death. John "Jake the Barber" Factor, brother of cosmetics magnate Max Factor, stock swindler, and front for the Chicago Syndicate, took over. Though he didn't live long enough to relish it, the fabulous Stardust lived up to Cornero's dream.

**More than five hundred people attended Tony Cornero's funeral. The FBI hired local photographer Dick Whittington to photograph the license plates of the more than fifty Cadillacs parked on the street.**

NOIR AFLOAT

**NIGHT FINAL** LATEST NEWS **5¢**

# EVENING ~ OUTLOOK

Westwood Hills Outlook

VOL. 80—NO. 182          SANTA MONICA, CALIFORNIA, MONDAY, AUGUST 1, 1955          West Los Angeles Tribune

# TONY CORNERO DROPS DEAD AT DICE TABLE

117
S.S. REX

Relentless

# PART II
# THE OTHER FLOATING CASINOS

NOIR NFLONT

# Introduction

The amazing adventure of gambling ships started in 1927, before Tony Cornero Stralla came on the scene, and ended in 1939, when California Attorney General Earl Warren closed them down. During that period as many as ten different gambling ships operated along the Southern California coastline, not all at the same time but intermittently over the years. Usually two or four might be in operation at one time at various places along the coast. When a gambling ship was lost by fire or by sinking or when it closed down, another came and replaced it.

Since each vessel was originally built for an entirely different purpose but later converted to a floating gambling casino, no two were alike. Each was operated in its own way and each had its own personality depending on the ships and who the owners were. Some experienced exciting lives because of robberies and murders while others, run by gangsters and Mafia members, cheated unsuspecting gamblers with rigged games. If one was lucky enough to win, most likely he would be robbed by a ship employee shortly after he got off the water taxi on shore.

The men who created and operated the gambling ships were persistent, creative, rich, and relentless. They knew there were plenty of gullible people who could not resist the urge to gamble and they took advantage of that. The gamblers who came for the most part were naive and foolishly under the impression they could beat the professional gamblers at their own game. Not only did they not beat them, they made them incredibly rich.

On the other hand, other customers took advantage of a free pass offering a free three-mile water taxi ride to the gambling ship, then enjoyed a free drink, a complementary dinner, and dancing. If they resisted the urge to put a nickel in a slot machine they came home from an exciting evening at a floating casino without spending a dime.

The operators believed what they were doing was legal and had enough money to hire the best lawyers to fight the authorities who wanted to put them out of business. They managed to fight them off for a while but in the end California Attorney General Earl Warren emerged the winner.

The following is a brief description of each of the other gambling ships that operated during this amazing period of California gambling ship history.

**The gambling-ship operators knew the odds were in their favor, yet many of them still elected to rig their games. Throngs of people came anyway, lured by the hope of beating the house.**

The first news reports of gambling on board a stationary vessel off the shores of Southern California appeared in newspapers on July 8, 1927. They were generated by a raid on a dingy, unimpressive-looking, flat-bottom fishing craft, known simply as *Barge C-1*. *Barge C-1* could usually be found anchored in Santa Monica Bay some four miles off Venice, just south of Santa Monica.

Authorities got wind of a shed erected on the deck of *Barge C-1* that contained a roulette wheel and poker tables. Los Angeles County Sheriff William Traeger authorized the raid based on District Attorney Asa Keyes's insistence that the barge's location was within the boundaries of the county. Early in the evening of July 7, a posse of six deputies from the sheriff's office headed out to sea with orders to board *Barge C-1*, put a stop to the gambling, arrest those responsible for it, and see that the vessel was closed down.

The barge's operators had apparently been tipped off to all of this in advance, and the police boat swooped down on nothing more untoward than some peaceful fishermen lining the rails with fishing poles and bait boxes. When the deputies entered the shed they found Fred U. Baggs, who identified himself as manager and operator of *Barge C-1*, and Art Gregory, a Venice salesman, at the roulette wheel, with $101.25 in cash laying nearby. The posse confiscated the illicit equipment and the cash and arrested both men. They were ferried back to the Santa Monica jail to be held on gambling charges. Far from going quietly, Baggs loudly declaimed that Los Angeles County had no jurisdiction in waters beyond the three-mile limit, and that the "gendarmes of France had as much right to arrest them as the county sheriff!"

Up to that point, the owner of *Barge C-1* was unknown, but shortly thereafter, Tutor Scherer of Los Angeles's Spring Street Gang stepped forward and identified himself as sole owner. Scherer denied authorities' statements that the barge's gambling operation was run by a syndicate, and that huge sums of money changed hands on board. Scherer claimed he alone had invested fifteen thousand dollars in the venture and was making barely one hundred dollars a week from it. It was never reported when he had installed the equipment or for how long it had been in use before the raid.

On July 21, 1927, both the *Santa Monica Evening Outlook* and the *Los Angeles Times* reported that Scherer had petitioned in U.S. District Court for a restraining order against District Attorney Keyes and Sheriff Traeger, and that Judge E.J. Henning had ordered the two men to appear before him and show cause why they should not be so restrained. On August 2, the *Los Angeles Times* reported that a U.S. District judge refused to act on Scherer's petition "on the grounds that it was not within federal jurisdiction to restrain county officers from performing

*Barge C-1* was California's first floating gambling casino. A roulette wheel and poker tables set up in one of its sheds offered the fishermen a chance to lose more than their bait.

their duty." Furthermore, the judge ruled that *Barge C-1*'s location was indeed within county limits, since federal jurisdiction in the area of Santa Monica Bay began not three miles from shore, but three miles from an imaginary line drawn between Point Vicente and Point Dume. Nevertheless, the matter seemed to melt away. Baggs and Gregory were never prosecuted As a result, no clear test case regarding jurisdiction in offshore waters that constituted part of a bay reached the courts, and no legal precedent was established. Nevertheless, gambling on *Barge C-1* was voluntarily shut down by her operator on the night of the raid, and she remained closed.

Registration papers show *Barge C-1* continued working from 1939 to 1965 as a legitimate barge for four different owners until she was scrapped. In 1965, National Metal and Steel Corporation, located at Terminal Island, bought and scrapped the forty-two-year-old barge.

*Barge C-1* set the scene for the arrival of a new element of Southern California crime that would prove to be a thorn in the side of reformers and law enforcement officials for years to come.

The lumber schooner *Johanna Smith* carried 1,500,000 board feet of lumber in Coos Bay, Oregon.
*Below:* The *Johanna Smith* was converted to a gambling ship and anchored beyond the three-mile limit off Long Beach.

NOIR AFLOAT

# *Johanna Smith*
## (1928-1932)

In the summer of 1928, a year after Tutor Scherer's gambling operation onboard fishing *Barge C-1* was shut down, a ship devoted entirely to gambling dropped anchor slightly beyond three miles off the shoreline, west of Long Beach. Credit for this first true Southern California gambling ship belonged to Clarence Blazier. Blazier purchased an aging steam schooner, the *Johanna Smith*, and had her converted into a far different environment than any flat-bottom barge could have provided. Blazier would own and operate more gambling ships—and be in business longer—than any of his counterparts. Initially, however, Blazier chose to keep his gambling enterprise under wraps.

The *Johanna Smith* was first launched at North Bend, Oregon, in 1917. She was the first steam schooner specifically designed to carry packaged lumber. She was owned by Pillsbury and Curtis, a California corporation based in San Francisco, which put her in service to its subsidiary, Pacific States Lumber. By 1927, having outlived her usefulness, the *Johanna Smith* was put up for sale. On January 10, 1928, Blazier agreed to purchase her, "as is" and without warranty, for $7,500.

A month later, when the transaction was formally recorded, the bill of sale listed Albert Howard, not Clarence Blazier, as the buyer. In itself this was not unusual. Ship owners would often hire an agent to purchase vessels for them. Howard was no ordinary agent, though; he was one of Blazier's front men. In return for taking title to the *Johanna Smith*, he was given a one-thousandth interest in the ship, plus a salary of two hundred dollars per month—a significant sum at the time.

When the *Johanna Smith* ran afoul of the law, it was Howard alone who dealt with the authorities, insisting the ship was entirely his, and never revealing the identity of her primary profiteers. By that time, they would include Blazier, Blazier's brother Ed, ex-rumrunner Marvin "Doc" Schouweiler, Ed V. Turner, and Herbert Sousa—all affiliated in one way or another with Los Angeles's Spring Street Gang.

Extensive refurbishing was necessary if the aging lumber schooner was to be rendered suitable for a new career. This transformation was carried out at Long Beach at a cost of fifty thousand dollars. Upon completion, she was towed by tug to her new anchorage at Long Beach in time for a July 1 opening. Although advance newspaper advertisements described her as a cabaret ship with a cafe and dancing pavilion, it was no secret that wide-open gambling was the *Johanna Smith's* most exciting feature. To the dismay and indignation of the city leeward of her, she became a success overnight.

Long Beach, located in southwest Los Angeles County, became a municipality in 1888. It was

*Johanna Smith*

"JOHANNA SMITH"
WORLD'S MOST FAMOUS
GAMBLING SHIP. W.M.S. ©

founded and populated by religiously conservative Methodists, and its very first ordinance outlawed saloons and gambling. Forty intervening years had done little to alter its civic and religious values. On the national scene, Methodists, who had been a driving force for Prohibition, denounced gambling as fervently as they preached temperance. Not surprisingly, the upstanding citizens of Long Beach were outraged over what they saw as the immoral, not to mention illegal, presence of the *Johanna Smith* in their vicinity, and they demanded that the ship be closed down. Accordingly, the City Council ordered Long Beach City Attorney Nolan Reid to rid the area of the *Johanna Smith* without delay. Yet gamblers came by the thousands to Long Beach and gladly parted with fifty cents for a round trip by water taxi to the *Johanna Smith* and the opportunity to risk their money

**Souvenir postcards were popular advertisements for the gambling ship.**

I enjoyed the cool ocean breeze when I visited the world famous pleasure ship JOHANNA SMITH Cabaret Dining Dancing Table d'Hote $1 Dinner No Cover Charge Fast Speed Boats leave dock every 15 minutes at 1415 West 7th St. Long Beach California

in her slot machines or, for higher stakes, at her roulette and craps tables.

As time went by, other gambling ships would appear off the coast, and Southern California newspapers would begin referring to them as "floating hellholes" and "sucker ships," terms that apparently had no deterrent effect whatsoever on the crowds that patronized them. On the contrary, such scurrilous terms only enhanced their aura of mystery and intrigue, arousing people's curiosity, and drawing more customers.

Clarence Blazier had been certain the *Johanna Smith* would make him and his partners a fortune, and she seemed to be on a fast track to that goal. Even more hands than those of the Spring Street Gang were in the

*Johanna Smith*

THE WORLD'S MOST FAMOUS
GAMBLING SHIP
*Johanna Smith*

GET SPEED BOATS AT
1415 WEST 7th STREET
Long Beach, Calif.

**$100 IN GOLD**
Given Away Every
Monday Evening
**FREE DRAWING**

FIRST PRIZE - - $50.00
SECOND PRIZE - - $25.00
THIRD PRIZE - - $15.00
FOURTH PRIZE - - $10.00

**KEEP THIS COUPON**

YOU DO NOT HAVE
TO BE PRESENT

SIGN THIS STUB
AND DEPOSIT IN BOX

Name ............................
Address .........................
City ............................
Phone ...........................

№ 163045

*Entertainment*

**SPORTIVE
GAMES**
and Other
Amusements
*WORLD FAMOUS*

New

**JOHANNA
SMITH!**

Under Same Management Since 1928

**Anchored in
smooth waters
off Long Beach**

**Fast Water Taxi
Leaves From
1315 West 7th
St., Long Beach
Every 15 Minutes**

Round Trip 25c • Open
1 P. M. Daily • Telephone
Long Beach 611-284

**DANCING**
Deluxe Dinner $1.00
Luncheon .... 50c
NO COVER CHARGE

The interior of the *Johanna Smith* was
unpretentious compared to its predecessors.
Her ivory chips were distinctive. Customers
responded to her straightforward
advertisements.

At first, the water taxis departed for the *Johanna Smith* from the double-decked Pine Avenue pier at Long Beach. The city denied use of its pier for that purpose, forcing the water taxis to move to the P&O dock, a private pier at 501 Pico Avenue.

pie, including the brothers William and Russell Sheffler, who operated a vending machine business in Los Angeles from 1915 to 1940. For a share of the machines' profits, the Shefflers leased Mills Silent Golden Slot Machines for use on the *Johanna Smith*.

Pressured by the populace and by civic promoters, Long Beach public officials and law enforcers quickly determined to take decisive action against the *Johanna Smith* and her operators, but just as quickly discovered themselves at a loss as to how to proceed. Both Long Beach and Los Angeles County had anti-gambling ordinances on their books, but in neither case did these contain any provisions applicable to gambling ships. A section of the California State Penal Code contained a clause making it a misdemeanor to take a person to a location where gambling was in progress, but the statute applied only within the borders of California, and the *Johanna Smith* was anchored in federal waters, outside the state's jurisdiction. The federal government had passed no legislation against gambling in federal territory.

Frustrated and increasingly harried, Long Beach authorities decided to focus on the water taxis. They

*Johanna Smith*

Federal agents Vincent Mangerina, left, Morey Tovel, center, and Joseph Seaman, pose at a roulette table after the raid and capture of the *Johanna Smith*, which put the ship out of business.

NOIR AFLOAT

reasoned that without their services, the *Johanna Smith's* owners would find the ship too expensive to operate. Their strategy was far from ideal, however, since the water taxis were a legitimate business. Water taxis were licensed by the State of California and the Long Beach Department of Recreation and had a legal function as fishing boats and sightseeing craft, free to travel to any location. No regulations required that they declare their destinations. Trying to close down an illegitimate operation by interfering with or impeding the activity of a legitimate one—much used and enjoyed by the public at large—would be a long shot at best. Nevertheless, it was agreed that some immediate and reportable action had to be taken, if only to fend off taxpayers' complaints that civic officials were failing them.

Accordingly, two days after the *Johanna Smith's* spectacular opening, Long Beach police raided the city-owned Pine Avenue Pier, from which taxis chartered by the ship from the P & O Water Taxi Company were transporting patrons to and from her. They tore down posted advertisements for the "cabaret ship," ordered the cessation of all ticket sales, and arrested eight boatmen on charges of soliciting for gambling games. Long Beach harbor commissioners followed through by prohibiting the use of harbor property as an embarkation site for people whose destination was a gambling vessel.

All this only briefly inconvenienced the *Johanna Smith's* operators and eager clientele. The taxis simply shifted their operations to the P & O Company's privately owned dock at the foot of nearby Fifth Street. A rueful Long Beach chief of police found himself having to tell the press: "The boatmen are licensed by the state, as well as the city, and there is nothing in the code that gives us the power to regulate their destination." Seeking federal help, investigators approached the United States Customs Office in nearby San Pedro to determine the validity of the *Johanna Smith's* registration and clearance papers. There they learned that Albert Howard had obtained a license from the Customs Office at San Francisco allowing the ship to work in the coasting trade for one year, that the *Johanna Smith* was not required to enter any port, and thus had not been cleared for any port and was free to anchor offshore. Further, since she was of American registry and carried an American crew, she was at liberty to cruise up and down the coast, anchoring at will.

Meanwhile, Chief Detective George Contreras and Fred Heaton from the Long Beach vice detail had taken a water taxi out to the *Johanna Smith*. They were determined to see for themselves what was taking place aboard her and were ready to arrest those in charge. To their chagrin, they discovered the ship was actually anchored off Orange County shores, rather than those of Los Angeles County, and was thus outside their jurisdiction.

Contreras, accompanied by a representative from City Attorney Reid's office, went to see Samuel W. McNabb, the United States attorney for the Southern District of California, to plead for assistance. McNabb explained that the problem Contreras was seeking to solve was of no concern to his office "because there is no federal law that prohibits gambling." He added that since the ship strictly banned liquor, there was no action he could take under the Eighteenth Amendment. However, he agreed to look into the matter to take action if it was found the *Johanna Smith* was in any violation of maritime law or posed a menace to navigation.

Long Beach officials next tried to shut the *Johanna Smith* down based on safety issues. They claimed

*Johanna Smith*

NOIR AFLOAT

she carried an inadequate number of lifeboats and life preservers. They asked federal steamship inspectors to board and inspect her. The inspectors replied that before the ship had been cleared for southern waters, the certificate of inspection issued to her in San Francisco had been "taken away." Without the certificate, the *Johanna Smith* could not legally move under her own power, but a tug could take her to any destination, and as long as she remained anchored at sea, the loss of her certificate was "irrelevant." An appeal to the United States Coast Guard proved equally fruitless, if somewhat less puzzling: "No violation of Prohibition, so no basis for interference."

The *Johanna Smith* continued to be a major popular attraction, and her operators believed her to be functioning completely within the letter of the law. A number of assistant United States attorneys, challenged by a situation in which government at all levels had reached a total impasse in its efforts, found what they were after in an obscure 135-year-old law, long in disuse. Enacted in 1792 as Section 4377 of the Revised Statutes of the United States, it authorized the federal government to seize any ship found to be in violation of her license. The *Johanna Smith*, licensed for coastal trade, was being used for other purposes.

Federal authorities now moved swiftly. They decided to seize the *Johanna Smith*, and they put United States Deputy Marshal Vincent C. Mangerina in charge of the action, with Deputy Marshals Morey Tovil and Joseph R. Seaman assisting. On August 23, 1928, carrying seizure orders, the deputy marshals headed for the *Johanna Smith*, with a boatload of newsmen close behind. The first person they encountered as they boarded the ship was employee Joe Sweitzer, to whom Mangerina declared: "The United States Government has seized this ship." His fellow deputies started tacking seizure notices on the bulkheads, as news photographers recorded the action. Sweitzer's attitude was belligerent. When a *Los Angeles Times* photographer snapped his picture, he promptly grabbed the camera and smashed it. Blustering, Sweitzer offered one hundred dollars in cash to anyone who would throw a photographer overboard. No one took him up on the offer. The newsmen finished their shots, climbed aboard the water taxi, and sped for shore.

Albert Howard then appeared on deck, surrounded by members of the *Johanna Smith*'s crew, and claimed to be the vessel's owner. Refusing to acknowledge the marshals' authority, he demanded that they get off the ship. A vociferous argument ensued, and fistfights or worse seemed imminent. The crewmen on the tug *Louie Black*, standing by to tow the *Johanna Smith* back to Long Beach, heard the commotion and called the U.S. Coast Guard on their newly installed radiotelephone. Coast Guard patrol boat *Arrow* responded at once, and fifteen armed Guardsmen climbed aboard the gambling ship in time to quell any serious violence.

Assessing the situation, the Coast Guard personnel took control of the *Johanna Smith* and started to prepare her for towing. They found it impossible to hoist the anchors. The crew had disabled the winches by removing bolts and other critical parts and tossing them overboard. With its armed men still in charge of the vessel, the Coast Guard called for a ship with a derrick to do the job.

Thirty-six hours later, tugs were finally able to take the once honest and hardworking lady in tow and

**Opposite:** The **Johanna Smith** settled into the mud at a remote spot in the harbor before she was pumped out and re-floated.

haul her to the Los Angeles harbor, where she was temporarily moored to Dock 92.

On November 24, 1928, Judge Henning handed down his decision, ruling that the seizure of the *Johanna Smith* had been lawful, and that she now belonged to the U.S. Government and would be sold at auction to the highest bidder on condition she be used "for legal purposes only." On December 14, now classified as an "illegitimate derelict," she went on the auction block at Berth 36 in the West Basin. Among those aboard her at the time were members of the Spring Street Gang, none of whom took part in any of the bidding. They were, however, seen to be in frequent conversation with a man by the name of Louis Fulvic.

In the course of the day, all the ship's furnishings and equipment were auctioned off. Four roulette tables, six dice tables, and a wheel of fortune went to the Ellis Mercantile Company of Los Angeles, for a total bid of $135. That company's representative stated that they would be used as "motion picture properties." When the bidding for the *Johanna Smith* herself reached its peak, the auctioneer, a U.S. marshal, brought his gavel down hard on the surface of a dice table and called out "Sold! for nine thousand dollars!" The winning bid was that of Louis Fulvic, who announced he would convert the vessel to a fishing barge. The money for his purchase had been put up by the Spring Street Gang gambling syndicate.

Time passed and the *Johanna Smith* languished in the harbor slowly settling in the mud. With her bilge pumps shut down she gradually filled with seawater. Harbor authorities ordered her pumped out and re-floated because she was becoming a menace to navigation. Her owners re-floated the vessel and fixed her up. They removed her propeller, thus converting her into a barge with no means of self-propulsion. This meant there was no need for registration or documentation or to apply for a license. They simply described her as a fishing barge and a floating café.

On June 25, 1929, a tug towed the *Johanna Smith* into Santa Monica Bay, where she anchored off of Venice. Records show she left San Pedro devoid of any gambling equipment. But by the time she arrived off Venice she was fully loaded with roulette wheels, dice tables, and other gambling devices apparently loaded en route. Perhaps because the *Johanna Smith* had carried a reputation for cleaning out her customers while operating in Long Beach, business was poor for her in Venice. Even over the Fourth of July, only slightly more than a hundred patrons came aboard, and most of those came only to look around.

Seeking a better turnout, the owners towed the barge some forty-three miles up the coast to Ventura. Being a farming community, the turnout was sparse. Only about three hundred came aboard, most not to gamble, but merely to see what a floating gambling casino looked like. The next stop was Point Mugu, where they used a private pier owned by Frank Kobode, located at a Japanese fishing camp. The sheriff told Kobode that if he continued to let the gambling ship use the pier he would condemn the whole camp as a public nuisance. He reacted to the sheriff's threat immediately and closed his pier to the speedboats. The *Johanna Smith* returned to Long Beach and anchored about a mile and one-half from two other gambling ships called the *Monte Carlo* and the *Rose Isle*.

On July 18, well after midnight there was a murder on the *Rose Isle*, and four days later the *Johanna Smith* caught fire. At 6 P.M. on July 22, 1932, well before the usual summer night crowd had assembled in her casino, some 110 patrons and crew members of the gambling ship were startled by the cry of "Fire! Someone set the ship on fire!" Seconds later, dense smoke rapidly filled the huge game room, and panic set in. Terrified customers—and some crew members as well—rushed for the open deck. Clarence Blazier lingered in the casino and gathered all available cash from tables and safes before joining the others.

As flames shot up from one end of the ship to the other, hands from a water taxi that had been puttering alongside rescued most of the hysterical passengers. Others crowded into a single lifeboat or were rescued by speedboats that had rushed to help. A dozen of the ship's crewmen stayed behind to fight the blaze, but jumped overboard to save their lives when the gasoline stores exploded. The nearby *Rose Isle*, empty of customers since the recent shooting, launched a lifeboat just in time to save them. There were no serious injuries and no lives lost. If the fire had erupted just a few hours later than it did, several hundred people would have been aboard and the story would have had a tragically different ending.

Transported to either the *Rose Isle* or the *Monte Carlo*, some shaken survivors of the *Johanna Smith* watched their chosen source for an evening of pleasure become completely engulfed in flames. Strangely, the Coast Guard had received no distress call from the ship when the fire began. Only when the water taxi brought its load of rescued passengers back to shore did the Guard learn what had occurred. By then, although four cutters and two Navy fireboats were sent out, the conflagration was utterly out of control, and the streams of water directed at it were of no avail. Spectators lined the shore to watch the spectacular fire with billowing black smoke reaching for the sky. The awful spectacle continued for almost three hours. When the flames finally died down, the *Johanna Smith* was only a charred hull, still attached to her anchors. The next morning's issue of the *Long Beach Sun* contentedly reported:

> Gamblers' gold turned to molten metal and ashes amid roaring flames that last night devoured
> the *Johanna Smith*, sending the Ship Without a Country to the Port of Lost Ships.

From San Diego, Coast Guard cutter *Shoshone* arrived in San Pedro Bay, carrying a team of demolition experts and a supply of bombs, for the purpose of destroying the *Johanna Smith's* remains before they became a menace to navigation.

"Arson Suspected," "Employees Attribute Blaze to Revenge Plot," and "Officers Puzzled" read the headlines of the *Long Beach Press-Telegram*. Police had suspected for some time that gang rivalry between the operators of the *Rose Isle* and the *Johanna Smith* was on the increase, and they believed the murder on the *Rose Isle* had been in some way connected to it. The insistence by multiple *Johanna Smith* employees that the fire had broken out simultaneously at her bow and stern, with others claiming it had started in three places at once—bow, carpentry shop, and stern—confirmed their conviction that it had been no accident. Indeed, some crew members specifically opined that *Rose Isle* part-owner and Mafioso Johnny Roselli had masterminded the disaster.

This tragic event marked the end of the old steam lumber schooner *Johanna Smith*.

*Johanna Smith*

# *Monfalcone*
## (1928-1930)

The *Monfalcone* began her life as a five-masted barkentine, the last of a series of fourteen such big wooden vessels intended for World War I service. She was built in Orange, Texas, in 1919 and ultimately launched well after the armistice marking the end of World War I. The *Monfalcone* displayed a discouraging penchant for getting caught in storms, and at one point she managed to run aground on the Atlantic seaboard. In 1923, en route to Panama, the unfortunate vessel sailed into a West Indian hurricane that stripped away her fore and top masts and swept her deck load of a thousand barrels of resin into the Gulf of Mexico.

Too crippled to proceed further on her own, the *Monfalcone* was hauled by tug through the Panama

The five-masted barkentine *Monfalcone* tied up at the San Pedro Lumber Company dock, waited to be converted to a gambling ship.

136

The sinister-looking *Monfalcone* anchored off Long Beach, looking more like an abandoned derelict than a lively gambling casino.

Canal and on to the Los Angeles harbor at San Pedro. Once back on land, her crew sued for unpaid wages, and a United States marshal sold her at auction to pay off their claims.

The *Monfalcone* disappeared from ship registration and enrollment lists and was not heard of again for more than four years. In February 1928, she turned up as a fishing barge anchored off Manhattan Beach, California. On October 1 of that year, according to United States Customs records at San Pedro, the *Monfalcone* was purchased jointly by J.W. "Jim" Byrnes, H.O. "Doc" Dougherty, Nick D. Oswald, Isadore Bernson, and Jack I. Dragna.

Although all of these men were known gamblers and racketeers, Jack Dragna—head of the Mafia in Southern California—was the most notorious. Two of his henchmen, Johnny Roselli and Charles Fischetti, both hard-core gangsters out of Chicago, would carry out his orders involving the *Monfalcone*.

Newspaper accounts of the cost of converting the *Monfalcone* varied from $68,000 to $100,000, and one described her as "equal to the best of any of the Mexican [gambling] resorts." Her owners proclaimed her a "gambler's heaven." Shipping men had other opinions. They warned that the *Monfalcone* was unsafe. "The owners," they said, "spent thousands of dollars fixing her up, but didn't spend a dime to make her seaworthy. In a storm, she would be a straw in the wind."

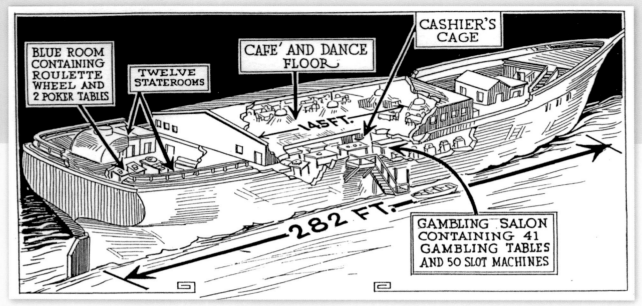

This artist's illustration defines the interior layout of the *Monfalcone*.

On the evening of November 24, 1928, the new *Monfalcone*, anchored a little over six miles from the Los Angeles harbor, held a gala opening attended by about five hundred patrons. One after another, water taxis from the P & O dock in Long Beach drew up alongside her brilliantly lit landing platform. A corps of waiters in ship's uniforms greeted boarding passengers and assisted them on board. Excited and curious customers climbed a steep flight of stairs to the main deck and entered the café and dance hall, from which a grand staircase descended to the gambling scene below deck.

Tommy Jacobs, owner of the Ship Café in Venice, California, ran the *Monfalcone*'s dining concession. He described his surroundings as an "arched paradise." Decorated in green and gold, the elegant café and dancing salon boasted a 125-foot matched hardwood floor, upon which guests could dance to the music of a seven-piece orchestra. Although he made a point of insisting that his dining concession had nothing whatsoever to do with the ship's gambling activities, Jacobs nevertheless enthusiastically predicted there would soon be a veritable breakwater of gambling ships extending from San Diego in the south to Santa Barbara in the north. "There is nothing," he crowed happily, "that the law can do to stop us!"

The *Monfalcone*'s gambling salon, two hundred feet long, occupied the entire area below the main deck. In her bow section were eight dice tables and sixteen blackjack games. Four roulette tables ran aft down her center, leaving ample room for twenty chuck-a-luck tables and money wheels, five poker tables, and fifteen slot machines.

One of the ship's owners, Jim Byrnes, formerly of the Foreign Club (a well-known Tijuana gambling house), managed the games on board and acted as official host and guide by day. Another of her owners, Doc Dougherty, supervised the night shift with the aid of sixty attendants.

The *Monfalcone*'s owners described her as a "sure thing" ship and her gambling casino as "luck proof." Gamblers who thought they stood a fair chance of winning big were in for a surprise. It was eventually discovered that dice players were rolling their dice on magnetic tables, and that the chuck-a-luck games were wired. Such arrangements were described by the proprietors as insurance—to keep a lucky gambler's winnings to a minimum.

A roulette table was usually worked by several dealers in rotating shifts. One of them would know how to rig the wheel. Managers would see to it that the right dealer was at the wheel if there was need to prevent it from stopping at numbers on which gamblers had bid heavily.

If a gambler did win a large sum, he would often be paid with counterfeit bills. Moreover, he would be at risk for robbery. According to one Los Angeles newspaper, a customer who had won

This artist's rendering shows the location of the *Monfalcone*. In this drawing, the bay points are depicted as Point Fermin on the north and Point San Juan Capistrano to the south. No accurate historical map has ever indicated that San Pedro Bay extended as far south as San Juan Capistrano. Whoever drew this map had no idea where the true bay points for San Pedro Bay were located. Those true bay points later became an important matter in court.

$501 on the *Monfalcone* noticed two men following him off the ship. Fearful, he asked the water taxi skipper to let him off at the P & O dock, instead of at Wilmington (in the Los Angeles harbor area), his usual point. Once ashore, he had walked only a block from the taxi when a small car overtook him and the same two men he had tried to evade got out. One shoved a gun into the unlucky fellow's ribs, while the other relieved him of his winnings, leaving him four dollars "for breakfast." The victim never knew whether they were gambling ship employees ordered to follow him and retrieve the money, or thieves trailing winners back to shore in order to rob them. In any event, the incident added greatly to the *Monfalcone*'s growing reputation as a sucker ship.

To thwart the law, owners of the *Monfalcone* had applied for and obtained pleasure-craft papers. Such papers stated that she would be used for fishing, dancing, and other forms of entertainment. With such a classification, no license was necessary. Moreover, the masterminds of the *Monfalcone*, anticipating the police would attempt to cut their taxi lifeline, took evasive action. They placed a legitimate fishing barge, the *Blue Sea*, about a mile to leeward of their ship. Water taxis ferried passengers only as far as the *Blue Sea*. Those wishing to go on to the gambling ship moved from the *Blue Sea* to another boat, which carried them to the *Monfalcone*. Plying only between the barge and floating casino, that boat carried no passengers from shore to ship.

For their part, taxi drivers at the P & O docks feigned total ignorance of this ploy. When questioned, one of them replied:

> What's all this about a gambling ship? These taxis are taking fishermen to the fishing barge
> *Blue Sea*, and as far as I know these people are fishermen and if they change ships out there
> I don't know anything about it!

**Monfalcone** is nearly ready for her debut at sea as a gambling ship.

On December 10, 1928, it became apparent that the *Monfalcone*'s transformation had not rid her of the bad luck that had always been her trademark. Once again she was caught in a storm, and by ten o'clock that night gale force winds were unmercifully pounding both her and her intermediary, the *Blue Sea*.

Earlier in the evening, the skipper of the *Blue Sea*, Captain H.W. Majors, had realized the severity of the approaching tempest and ordered all passengers aboard his barge to head for shore. Water taxis carried them back to the P & O dock, while the skipper and four of his crew remained on board to ride out the storm. His account of the terrifying ordeal that followed was published in the *Los Angeles Examiner*:

> Huge waves began breaking over us and flooded out our dynamos, so that our signal lights on the masts were extinguished. We had been trying to call for help with these. Then we managed to build a fire on deck, in the hopes some vessel would see this and come to our rescue, but this was washed out quickly.
>
> At midnight a wave larger than the rest smashed us, and the *Blue Sea* broke in half. She was getting lower and lower by that time, and her decks were awash, with pieces of wood being swirled here and there and hitting up terrific blows.
>
> We had nothing to eat, of course and the worst of it was we couldn't even get a drink of fresh water after swallowing all the salt water of the waves. There was a three-hundred-gallon tank of fresh water on the *Blue Sea*, but we were unable to get at this.
>
> The small boat containing Lieutenant H.A. Burke and five sailors from the *Procyon* was the most welcome sight we ever saw as it came across the sea and took us aboard.

The terrified men of the *Blue Sea* had been clinging to her wreckage for fifteen hours. Their rescuers took them to the U.S.S. *Procyon*. Captain Majors, Charles Jameson, and Barry Dunham, the only survivors, were moved as quickly as possible to the hospital ship U.S.S. *Relief*.

That the wreckage of the *Blue Sea* drifted into the area it did was providential. The U.S. Navy's battleship fleet had been out at sea on gunnery maneuvers until the storm broke, when the maneuvers were canceled and the vessels ordered to return to port. Two of them passed within yards of the stranded men and neither saw nor heard them. Only one sailor, a lookout on the U.S.S. *Procyon*, spotted the debris on the waves and the pitiful figures clinging to the wreckage of their barge.

While the tragedy of the *Blue Sea* was well-covered in the local papers, little if any mention was made of the *Monfalcone*'s experience of the storm. What was reported was that Byrnes and Dougherty went out to the gambling ship the next day to check for damage and discovered that the *Blue Sea* was missing. They immediately contacted the Coast Guard, which sent two cutters to the site where the barge was usually anchored. All day they searched the vicinity for any sign of her or her crew. Only later did they learn, along with the story of her loss, that the wreckage of the *Blue Sea* at the time of her rescue had drifted some fifteen miles southeast of her regular location.

In 1930, Mafioso Jack Dragna became dissatisfied with owning a mere twenty-five percent interest in

*Monfalcone*

141

the *Monfalcone*, and decided he wanted total control of her operations as well. Opting as usual for immediate action, he sent five of his henchmen to take her over. Johnny Roselli and Charles Fischetti, together with "Russian Louie" Strauss and two other mobsters, boarded a taxi headed for the *Johanna Smith*. As soon as it passed the breakwater, all five men drew their guns and ordered the boatmen to take them to the *Monfalcone* instead.

Once on board the *Monfalcone*, the raiders fired their guns skyward, announced they were taking over the ship, and conferred briefly with Tommy Jacobs and Nick Oswald, who were handling her that evening. The conference ended with Jacobs and Oswald on their way back to shore. None of the 150 or more customers at the gaming tables, who had remained engrossed in play, had the slightest idea that anything untoward had taken place.

Back on land, Jacobs and Oswald at once called part-owner Jim Byrnes. Furious, Byrnes ordered his attorney to call the police to report the takeover and demand that they do something about it. In turn, the police contacted Deputy District Attorney David Clark, who had long been trying to find some way of getting rid of the ships, and got only ironic laughter in response to their request. The police did nothing, and from that point on, the Mafia were in full charge of the *Monfalcone*'s day-to-day business.

Early in the evening of August 30, 1930, aboard the *Monfalcone,* some 350 patrons were at play, while below decks the ship's engineer was repairing a leak in the line that fed gasoline to the engine that ran the ship's generator. Suddenly, sparks from the generator ignited fumes that had collected in the enclosed area, resulting in an explosion that caused nearby stores of oil and gasoline to burst into flames. The tremendous blast severely rocked the ship, and almost at once flames broke from her hold. Simultaneously, the lights went out, plunging her into total darkness.

The *Monfalcone*'s panic-stricken passengers rushed for the top deck. Miraculously, no one was trampled to death. Water taxis, excursion boats, and even a fishing craft sped to the scene of the conflagration and carried every person aboard the burning vessel safely to the *Johanna Smith*. The ship's engineer suffered severe second-degree burns, the cook was slightly burned, and a crewman bruised his leg attempting to lower a lifeboat. There were no other injuries. Had the disaster occurred only a few hours later, more than one thousand patrons would have been on board.

All along the coast from Huntington Beach to San Pedro, crowds watched the huge pyrotechnic display out on the water. Once out of danger, the rescued customers of the *Monfalcone* gradually achieved at least a semblance of calm. Some, thinking of worried relatives and friends ashore, departed for land as soon as taxis were available for the purpose. Others adopted a nonchalant attitude and resumed their play at the *Johanna Smith's* tables. By far the majority, however, crowded the *Johanna Smith's* rails, mutely watching the burning ship and, for the moment, thinking only of their narrow escape.

As for the old wooden barkentine, she was beyond saving. Within three hours, she had burned to her waterline, and only a black and smoldering skeleton of a vessel remained. The next morning, when a salvage ship preparing to tow her remains cut loose her anchor, the *Monfalcone*'s hull turned over and sank, taking with it anything on board that had not been incinerated by the blaze. She came to rest right side up on the ocean

**Following orders from the Coast Guard, two tugs pushed the *Monfalcone* into the harbor; she was declared a menace at sea.**

floor. At his own expense, because his fellow owners protested it as a useless effort, Tommy Jacobs had divers sent down to see if any money could be retrieved. They brought up two safes. One of them, which had contained some fourteen thousand dollars in cash and checks, was empty, its door hanging open. Jacobs recalled that the door had been open at the moment catastrophe struck. The other safe, which reportedly had been locked, with some forty thousand dollars inside, also came up empty and open-doored. A question arose as to whether it had been rifled during the first confused minutes after the blast. Jacobs, however, then allowed that he knew both had been unlocked, and the matter was dropped. In the end, only about fifteen hundred dollars in coins and "globs" of silver dollars that had melted into each other in the intense heat were retrieved. The *Monfalcone* had not been insured, and her owners ultimately reckoned the cost of her loss at $115,000. Undeterred by financial disaster, they at once began seeking a replacement ship.

*Monfalcone*

NOIR AFLOAT

# *Rose Isle*
## (1930-1935)

The vessel that took the *Monfalcone*'s place off the coast of Long Beach was thirty years older than her predecessor. Built in 1889 and named *Yumuri*, she spent her first nine years in service as a passenger ship in the South American trade. In 1898, the U.S. Navy purchased the *Yumuri*, renamed her the U.S.S. *Badger*, and put her to work as a naval auxiliary craft. Next, the Army took her over, turned her into a troop ship, and renamed her the U.S.Q.M.D. *Lawton*. She later went back to the Navy and was renamed the U.S.S. *Lawton*. In 1907, she was sold to the San Francisco and Portland Steamship Company, underwent a complete renovation, was re-christened the *S.S. Rose City* (in honor of the city of Portland, Oregon, her new home base), and returned to passenger service.

Subsequently, the McCormick Steamship Company acquired the S.S. *Rose City*, and she continued plying between Portland, San Francisco, and Los Angeles. In 1930, when financial reverses forced the McCor-

*Opposite:* **The steamer S.S. *Rose City* heads into the Los Angeles harbor when she was still an active passenger ship.**
*Below:* **Having been converted to a gambling ship in San Francisco, the *Rose Isle* is anchored off Long Beach.**

*Rose Isle*

**The walls were decorated with what appears to be pseudo Egyptian hieroglyphics. Gamblers try their luck at the Chuck-a-Luck table.**

mick line to suspend passenger service, she was withdrawn from service and relegated to the scrap heap. Despite her advanced age, the S.S. *Rose City* was not destined to rust away in a graveyard of ships. She was soon rescued from that fate by a dubious lot of Prince Charmings from the Los Angeles underworld. Her new owners were Tommy Jacobs and Dragna front-man Johnny Roselli (both from the late *Monfalcone*); Tutor Scherer (from the *Johanna Smith*); Milton "Farmer" Page (a part-owner of the *Johanna Smith* who had later purchased a fifteen-percent interest in the *Monfalcone*); William Gleason and Harry Belford, a name not previously identified as being associated with any gambling ship.

At a cost of more than $100,000, conversion of the S.S. *Rose City* into a gambling ship was completed in San Francisco. All passenger accommodations were removed and replaced by gaming rooms, dining rooms, and a dance floor. Although Jacobs described this new floating casino as depicting "a Roman gallery at the time of Emperor Caligula," her interior decoration was more pseudo-Egyptian than Roman, and her new name, the *Rose Isle*, seemed inappropriate to either style.

On October 5, 1930, tugs towed the *Rose Isle* from San Francisco to the waters off Long Beach, and shortly thereafter she was opened to the public. To attract customers, her proprietors mailed the following invitation to thousands of individuals, as well as businesses and other organizations:

> This invitation when presented to the head waiter in the dining room will defray all dinner expense for self and party.
>
> The *ROSE ISLE* offers release from everyday monotony by substituting romance and thrills. A speedy and dependable water taxi, swift and sure as a searchlight's ray, conveys you comfortably to the ship.
>
> Aboard you will find all the details modern ingenuity has devised for ease and comfort.
>
> The three decks of the *ROSE ISLE* are decks of increasing interest: boat deck, promenade deck, and "A" deck.

From the boat deck, as you recline in a snug deck chair, new vistas unfold in charming variety; thousands of shore lights and millions of overhead stars wink back their reflected radiance from the shimmering sea that lies peacefully before you.

The promenade deck entices you with an unbroken walkway over four hundred feet in length and as you stroll the soft strain of the ship's orchestra is a pleasing accompaniment.

The band played music for dancing, and its large variety of musical instruments allowed the musicians to supply almost any kind of sound.

The dining room—decorated in the modern manner—is on the promenade deck and has a spacious dancing floor; the cuisine needs no encomiums as it is justly famous.

The "A" deck, just below the promenade deck, is a deck of such unusual interest and fascination that any attempt to describe its charm and appeal would fail miserably to portray the many delightful diversions to be enjoyed there.

We are anxious to have you as our guest, at your convenience, and this invitation is sent to you in the hope that you will accept our hospitality in the same whole-hearted manner it is extended. You are at liberty to bring as many friends with you as you wish and to you and your party there will be no charge for music, dinner, or dancing.

Free parking space is available on the P & O Docks, 501 Pico Avenue, one block south of Seventh Street, Long Beach, Calif. The water taxis leave from the same dock.

Any special arrangement or further information may be had by telephoning Trinity 0441 and asking for the *ROSE ISLE* representative.

Such elegant wording and heartwarming tones, together with their promise that little or no expenditure would be required, would have been hard to resist in that first full year of the Great Depression. As usual, the issuers of the invitation had been circumspect—sure that only an utterly unworldly recipient would fail to

*Rose Isle*

understand that the "delightful diversions" on the "A" deck would turn out to be roulette wheels, craps games, and slot machines.

Moreover, the *Rose Isle* at night was indeed a grand sight, festooned as she was with thousands of sparkling lights reflected in the surrounding sea. Water taxi passengers' anticipation could only increase as the joyful strains of "Happy Days Are Here Again" reached them across the water, blaring out from loudspeakers mounted over her landing platform.

On November 29, 1930, Long Beach officials had had enough and launched a raid on the water taxis at the P & O dock, from which the *Rose Isle* was served. The raiders confronted heavy resistance from the taxi operators. The operator of the taxi *Bearcat* threw a vice squad officer into the harbor, and fought with another in their attempt to get away. A detective on board the taxi's upper deck jumped down to help, and the crew was finally subdued and handcuffed. At the West Seventh Street dock, the crew of the first boat raided, the *Mike*, refused to come ashore until police trained their guns on them.

The hundreds and hundreds of modishly dressed men and women lining the docks waiting transport to the *Rose Isle* watched checkers, starters, and even parking attendants herded into patrol wagons. Other hundreds of patrons were temporarily marooned on the *Rose Isle* when taxi crews, aware that a raid was under way, refused to carry them back to shore. They wound up having to charter a boat themselves.

In Los Angeles, as the year neared its close, District Attorney Buron Fitts and his staff were increasingly worried and restive. Well aware of the gambling ships' gang and Mafia connections, they had come to view the vessels as the visible tip of an otherwise hidden and amorphous criminal iceberg.

Long Beach had notified them that the *Rose Isle* was really controlled by a St. Louis mob, and newspapers were reporting that Capone agents had been spotted trying to buy up coastal ranches for use as liquor-landing sites. Advance notice of the *Los Angeles Examiner's* soon-to-be-released report that 1930 had produced the worst record of crime in the city's 149-year history was a further source of irritation. Gangland-type violence of the sort to endanger both law enforcement personnel and an innocent public seemed apt to erupt any day, and Fitts was convinced the floating casinos would be involved.

Sure enough, on the evening of December 21, a kidnapping conspiracy on the part of a group of mostly Eastern hoods against a Spring Street Gang member went violently and tragically awry in the dockside parking area used by patrons of the *Rose Isle*. The kidnappers included Ralph Sheldon, out of Chicago and a former Capone lieutenant; Jesse "Cheesey" Orsatti, another Chicago gangster and a murder suspect to boot; Ray Wagner, an ex-convict from St. Louis; Jimmy Doolin, a St. Louis gunman; Bill Bailey, from Detroit, wanted for robbery and burglary and once employed by Hollywood studios as an advisor on crime films; and Louis Frank, wanted back East and currently hiding out in a house in Sunland. Their Spring Street Gang victim was Ezekiel L. "Zeke" Caress, flamboyant and well-known millionaire gambler and Agua Caliente racetrack handicapper and betting commissioner.

On the previous evening, December 20, all six conspirators had abducted Caress, his wife, and his Japanese houseboy from the driveway of the gambler's Los Angeles mansion. They drove their captives to a bungalow near Alhambra and demanded a fifty-thousand-dollar ransom. Caress carried no such amount on him, and banks were closed for the weekend. Knowing only a gambling establishment would have that much money readily available, Caress wrote out four personal checks totaling fifty thousand dollars, payable to a friend by the name of Les Bruneman. His captors agreed Bruneman could take the checks to the *Rose Isle* where, Caress assured them, his good friend and fellow Spring Street Gang member Tutor Scherer would cash them and turn over the money.

At 7 P.M. on December 21, Sheldon, carrying the checks, accompanied by two of his co-conspirators, and driving a car borrowed from Bailey, picked up Bruneman at Sixth and Spring Streets in Los Angeles. The four men headed for Long Beach and impending disaster. None of them were aware that a detail of Long Beach police stationed at the *Rose Isle* parking area routinely stopped every car, simply to caution its occupants against going to the gambling ship.

The officers on duty that evening signaled Sheldon to stop and approached the car to issue their usual warning. As they did so, the mobsters, assuming the police had recognized them and suspected what they were up to, drew their guns and started shooting. Bullets narrowly missed Officers C.A. Jenks and J.E. Slaughter. But Officer W.H. Waggoner took a serious wound to his spine. Paralyzed, he would lie near death for months and ultimately be confined to a wheelchair for the rest of his life.

As police grabbed Sheldon, the car's three other occupants fled. One of the escapees later got word to the Alhambra hideout that "we had to scrub a cop!" Those left on guard there released their three captives and made a rapid getaway. Sheldon was arrested, and the four checks he had been carrying were seized as evidence, though of what the police were not sure. Owners of the *Rose Isle* later told investigators they would not have cashed them. A furious Buron Fitts ordered Sheldon held on three counts of assault with intent to commit murder. Soon afterward, Caress and his wife reported the kidnapping to the police, and the connection between the checks and the shootout became clear.

Within two days, a grand jury indicted Ralph Sheldon for assault with a deadly weapon with intent to kill and issued "John Doe" bills to cover his alleged confederates, none of whom had been captured. Sheldon was returned to jail in lieu of $100,000 bail. Deputy district attorneys went into a lengthy conference with both Los Angeles and Long Beach police officials, which ended in an agreement that all three agencies would work together to solve both crimes.

On Friday, December 26, 1930, a major manhunt began. Fitts was certain that some of the criminals at large would be hiding out on one or another of the gambling ships, and ordered immediate raids on the *Rose Isle* and the *Johanna Smith*. He set up a temporary headquarters in the Long Beach home of Deputy District Attorney William Brayton, from which he personally supervised the raids. That evening, heavily armed officers simultaneously raided both vessels—thirty boarding the *Rose Isle* and twenty-five the *Johanna Smith*.

On the *Rose Isle*, more than a hundred patrons fled the "A" Deck when Chief Investigator Blayney Matthews ordered the manager to cease all playing, adding, "You can either submit quietly or we'll shoot it out with you." No violence ensued, and after a search turned up no malingering gangsters, officers arrested seven

*Rose Isle*

men and confiscated a quantity of gambling paraphernalia. Those arrested were Tutor Scherer and William Gleason (on charges of operating a gambling place) and dealers George Webster, Homer Thompson, Frank Morie, Richard Elgin, and Fred Baggs (on charges of gambling). Doubtless Baggs did not mention that he was also a part-owner of the *Johanna Smith*. Later, when Scherer and Gleason each posted five hundred dollars bail, he and the other dealers had to come up with only one hundred dollars. All seven were to have a hearing in Los Angeles Municipal Court.

The simultaneous raid on the *Johanna Smith* developed differently. Although her manager made no show of resistance, he did produce a map that showed her as anchored on the high seas, beyond county jurisdiction, and on that ground he politely declined to be arrested. The officers searched the ship thoroughly for known gangsters, found none, and disembarked without making any arrests or seizing any gambling equipment.

Early the next day tugs appeared and towed each to a new location. One took the *Rose Isle* nearly three more miles out to sea, almost into the shipping lane, and the other towed the *Johanna Smith* a mile and one-half southeast to a point off Orange County. That evening, both floating casinos were doing business as usual at their new sites.

Fitts was not finished with the *Johanna Smith* by any means. Within hours of opening that day, with Brayton in charge and the Long Beach police department assisting, he went after both the ship and her shore connections (three Bearcat taxis from the West Seventh Street dock) with a vengeance. Early in the evening, police operatives posing as patrons boarded one of the taxis and went to the ship, where some of them engaged in gambling, returned to shore, arrested the taxi crew, and tied the boat up for the night. The other two Bearcats, with officers aboard, were sent to the ship to take everyone else off. The passengers had already been informed by officers who were still aboard that if they failed to leave in "one of the next two boats available", they would be held as material witnesses, and they were waiting frantically to be picked up. As those two boats returned to land, their crews were arrested, along with dealers, musicians, and other employees of the ship, as they stepped ashore. Holiday season crowds who had been waiting to go out to the *Johanna Smith* were turned back at the dock with a similar warning about otherwise being held as material witnesses.

Brayton announced that all people arrested would be held without bail from that Saturday night until the following Monday or Tuesday, December 29 or 30. The taxi operators were charged with conspiracy to violate state gambling laws and booked at Los Angeles County jail. The ship's employees were charged as material witnesses and booked at Long Beach city jail. Fitts also issued warrants for the arrest of Clarence Blazier and Ed V. Turner. All, according to the *Long Beach Press Telegram*, were to be arraigned in Los Angeles Municipal Court on New Year's Eve morning.

In all, seven men from the *Rose Isle* were out on bail pending a hearing in Los Angeles Court; thirteen employees of the *Johanna Smith* and four of her taxi operators were being held without bail pending a hearing in Los Angeles Court; and three warrants were out for the arrest of *Johanna Smith* operators Clarence Blazier and Ed V. Turner, and John Doe Allen, a person whose connection with the *Johanna Smith* was not clear, but whose name made the headline about her. On Monday, December 29, 1930, both the *Johanna Smith* and the *Rose Isle* were dark, and armed guards from Buron Fitts's staff patrolled the Long Beach waterfront to prevent either patrons or employees from riding out to them. Although the raids had turned up no fugitives from justice, they fulfilled at least one of the district attorney's stated intentions: "We will make life so miserable for the gamblers that they will cease operating their ships." As he was quick to point out, had those ships not been there in the first place, the shot that transformed Officer Waggoner from stalwart police officer to helpless cripple would never have been fired.

## Murder and Arson

What did startle the public into an increased awareness of the essentially dangerous nature of the floating casinos were two shocking events that occurred on gambling ship row—one on the *Rose Isle*, the other four nights later on the *Johanna Smith*—the summer of 1932. District Attorney Fitts's prediction that violence would sooner or later erupt on the gangster-ridden *Rose Isle* proved true.

Well after midnight on July 18, the after-hours quiet on the *Rose Isle* was shattered by the sound of gunshots. The shots came from a cabin in which three employees had been drinking and arguing. First to reach the scene was Dan O'Connor, a former St. Louis policeman turned ship's bouncer. Bursting into the little room, he found croupier Charles Bozeman lying on the floor and bouncer James O'Keefe and busboy Virgil Roach slumped over the cabin table, all apparently in a state of alcoholic stupor.

Deciding that Bozeman was the worst off of the three, O'Connor, as he later testified, proceeded to drag him out on deck into fresh air. In the process, O'Connor saw that Bozeman was severely wounded and bleeding heavily. Leaving him there, shoulders propped against the rail, O'Connor went for medical help.

The physician-owner of an emergency service on shore arrived by speedboat half an hour later. By that time, Bozeman had already bled to death from a bullet wound beneath his heart. The doctor returned to land at once and contacted the Coast Guard, then the Long Beach police. The former sent a boat to the *Rose Isle* immediately. Guardsmen boarded the ship and took control until the appropriate authorities could get there.

Bozeman, a former East St. Louis mob figure, whose brother was reportedly one of the *Rose Isle*'s owners, had been leading a double life aboard. He functioned as both a croupier and a fence for diamonds and other gems stolen in Los Angeles robberies. O'Keefe, also out of St. Louis, was a known racketeer and killer. Roach, so far as was known, was nothing more than a busboy.

Since the *Rose Isle* was anchored beyond the three-mile limit and hence in federal waters, the U.S. Justice Department agreed to handle the case. A team of federal investigators, assisted by a Long Beach police detective and an investigator from the district attorney's office, interviewed every one of the ship's employees. Fear of retaliation by the mob made it next to impossible for police to elicit any substantive information from the petrified crew.

*Rose Isle*

151

O'Keefe, who was being held in Long Beach city jail, insisted he had been sleeping in an adjacent cabin, was awakened by a disturbance outside, went to see what was going on, and found Bozeman lying on the deck. Roach, on the other hand, told investigators that he, Bozeman, and O'Keefe had been together in the cabin for hours, and that just before he passed out he heard two shots, but didn't see who fired them.

The team wound up with little more than a jumble of conflicting stories and no clues as to the motive for the killing. In the ship's cabin, however, Coast Guardsmen had found a gun belonging to O'Keefe on the floor, as well as three spent shells. O'Keefe was charged with the killing of Charles Bozeman, and Virgil Roach was held as a material witness. Justice Department attorneys asked a federal grand jury to indict O'Keefe for murder and piracy and went for a sentence of life imprisonment.

Under questioning at the ensuing trial, some *Rose Isle* employees changed their original statements, while others disclosed information that they had not previously mentioned. As a result, testimony was confusing. Nevertheless, members of the jury felt they had heard enough to reach a verdict, and they found the defendant guilty as charged. The judge, in whose opinion the evidence presented had been neither clear nor sufficient, disagreed with them. As a result, he sentenced O'Keefe to a mere five years in prison, with a concurrent five years' probation. Federal prosecutors made no objection and let the matter rest.

It was soon after this that the owners of the *Rose Isle* decided to leave the business. On August 2, 1932, the Olympics were getting under way and thousands of potential evening patrons were streaming into Long Beach for the rowing races. After the *Johanna Smith* had burned and her wooden remains were demolished by the Coast Guard, William Gleason announced the sale of the *Rose Isle* to Clarence Blazier and Harold Sousa, the owners of the late *Johanna Smith*. The amount Blazier paid was never made public. He renamed the *Rose Isle* the *Johanna Smith II* and let it be known that William Gleason would continue to manage her.

For the next three years the *Johanna Smith II* remained in business, suffering various problems with the authorities.

## Murder on the *Johanna Smith II*

Late on the night of September 20, 1933, Assistant U.S. Attorney William F. Palmer in Los Angeles was awakened by a call from the Long Beach police. There had been a shooting on the *Johanna Smith II*. No doctor was aboard, and the ship's operators had been bringing the unconscious victim to shore by water taxi when he expired. DOA at the West Seventh Street dock. What should they do?

Already reaching for his phone list of available agents, Palmer reacted instantly: "Get those guys back on their ship and don't let anyone off until our men get there. Should take about half an hour!"

The federal investigators Palmer called didn't need to be told to hurry. The killer was most likely still aboard the ship, and they needed to get there before any passenger disembarked. Meeting at downtown head-

An advertisement for the *Rose Isle*, left, appeared in the *Los Angeles Examiner* on August 11, 1932. The ad for the *Johanna Smith II* was published in the *Examiner* five days later. Clarence Blazier had purchased the *Rose Isle* after his gambling ship *Johanna Smith* caught fire and sank, so he changed the name of *Rose Isle* to *Johanna Smith II*.

quarters, the team piled into a car and headed south. By this time it was well past midnight, and the dense fog common in Southern California that time of year had rolled in from the sea, blanketing the entire coast. On all sides, the night had disappeared into a silent, eerie, and impenetrable whiteness. Visibility was zero. Headlights were useless. Sounds were muffled. The car crept along at a snail's pace, the driver stopping every now and again to get out and, senses straining, try to make sure they were still on the right road.

The twenty-four-mile trip to Long Beach plus the speedboat ride to the gambling ship took over two

harrowing hours. Nerves frayed, but still alert, the government agents—now accompanied by Long Beach police and detectives—boarded the *Johanna Smith II*. They were met by no fewer than 250 equally frustrated, angry, and weary patrons, none of whom had been given any information as to why they were being held. Also on board were the sixty-five employees.

The team had only one clue to work with. In searching the dead man, police had found a seaman's card bearing the name of Norman Lorraine. Investigators formed the crowd into two groups—passengers in one and employees in the other—and began asking the same three questions of everyone: Had he or she heard any gunshots? Did he or she know anyone named Norman Lorraine? Was anybody missing from his or her party? Nobody had heard any shots. Nobody knew anyone named Norman Lorraine. Nobody was missing.

Three of the ship's musicians, however, were able and willing to provide an account of relevant events that evening. The musicians recalled hearing gunshots. After hearing the shots, the musicians rushed topside in time to see one man hurrying away toward the aft end of the ship and another lying on the deck. The musicians ran for the captain, who arrived to find the prone figure still breathing. The captain ran to the crowded game room and commanded the drummer to play a drum roll to catch the attention of the crowd. He then called "Is there a doctor in the house!?" No one responded.

From the musicians' description of the hurrying figure, federal agents narrowed the number of possible suspects from 265 to seven. After a thorough search of the ship failed to turn up a weapon, they fingerprinted each of the seven suspects and made preparations for everyone to be taken back to land, one boatload at a time. The seven suspects were to wait for the last load. By then it was 6 A.M.

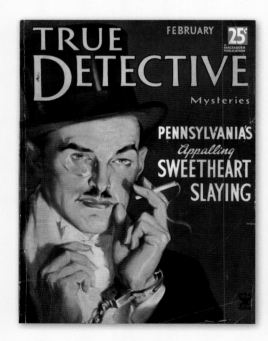

As the final batch of passengers, the seven possible suspects included, were getting into a water taxi under the watchful eyes of the feds, one young patron at the end of the line paused before descending to the landing platform. He turned and spoke softly to the ship's officer supervising the departure. Somewhat fearfully, he confided that he had just visited the restroom and, while there, had seen a cleaning attendant discover a gun behind one of the bowls. He had followed the ensuing action long enough to see the attendant turn the weapon over to a crew member, who simply ditched it under a nearby shoeshine stand. The officer nod-

**A murder on the *Johanna Smith II* in 1932 caused a sensation. Later, in February 1935, *True Detective* magazine published an article about the murder in which the author embellished the details.**

ded and let the young fellow continue down the ladder to the landing platform.

Shortly thereafter, the officer passed the information onto the investigators. The latter quickly deduced that the gun must have been cached in the restroom only moments earlier, and that its owner was thus aboard the last taxi, which by that time had untied from the ship and was on its way back to land. Two Long Beach detectives leaped into the speedboat they had come out in and went after the taxi at full throttle, catching up with it barely a boat's length from the dock. They turned it back and ordered its exhausted passengers back onto the *Johanna Smith II*. There, the investigators told them they would now have to fingerprint each one of them—except for the seven whose prints had been taken earlier. At this, one of the seven moved forward: "Why waste time? I did the killing. The fingerprints will match mine." Police took him in tow as the others headed once again for the water taxi, their night-long ordeal finally over. The following evening, the *Johanna Smith II* had virtually no customers.

The confessed killer was James Walsh, a twenty-four-year-old ex-convict and hardened criminal. The man he had killed was his partner in crime, Buell Dawson. The two had been planning to pull off several robberies and kidnappings. The name Norman Lorraine was an alias Walsh had used in the past. The seaman's card bearing it had been in the victim's possession because both men had recently been seeking work on the San Francisco waterfront with only the one card between them. They had agreed that whoever was hired first could use it, and Dawson had been carrying it when they gave up looking for jobs and came south.

Taken to Los Angeles for questioning, Walsh told a sordid and pathetic story. He and Dawson had been cellmates at Leavenworth Prison, both serving sentences for car theft. Released only a few months before, Walsh—who had already spent seven of his twenty-four years behind bars—was picked in July in Detroit as a "suspicious character." Police records there revealed he was wanted in San Francisco for mail theft. Escorted to that city, he had pleaded guilty, but he had

MURDER on the PROMENADE DECK

By MADELINE KELLEY

California's Great Gambling Ship Mystery

cunningly practiced reverse psychology on an apparently lenient judge by asking for a year in prison, explaining he feared he would commit a major crime otherwise. The judge instead put him on probation and even gave him permission to assume the alias of James Sullivan—the name he had originally given the federal investigators. Dawson, released from Leavenworth a month later, had joined Walsh in San Francisco.

Failing to find work immediately, the cohorts each bought a gun—Walsh in Sacramento and Dawson in San Jose. They traveled south by separate routes and rendezvoused on the Long Beach Pike on the morning of the shooting. Their primary concern was to finalize plans for a series of robberies as well as the kidnapping of oil magnate E.L. Doheny. Doheny was credited with discovering oil in Los Angeles and was known publicly for his extreme wealth. As the day wore on, they began drinking, took in a movie, and wound up the evening on the floating casino. While on board they continued an argument that had been going on between them off and on for hours. Its subject, as Walsh described it, was their respective "codes of life."

Dawson, said Walsh, was adamantly opposed to killing "anyone other than a cop" and had been repeatedly telling him he couldn't go along with Walsh's rule of "shooting [victims] if they don't come through." Around 11 P.M., as they were standing on the deck of the *Johanna Smith II*, Dawson escalated the dispute by threatening to turn Walsh in if he shot someone who was not a policeman. "Why, I'd just as soon kill you as anyone else," Walsh had retorted. "You're just a rat!" Suiting the action to the word, Walsh pulled his gun and fired five shots into Dawson's body.

In an attempt to establish that he had acted in self-defense, Walsh somewhat belatedly added that Dawson had been about to pull his own gun at the time. Investigators already knew, however, that the victim's coat had been completely buttoned at the time his body was discovered, and his gun was later found in its inside pocket. It would have been hard to find a better example of the type of character with which Buron Fitts insisted the gambling ships were infested. Walsh was arrested and charged with murder on the high seas. He was sent to McNeil Island Federal Prison for life.

As a result of this latest crime, public concern about the gambling ships began to swell. From all over the Southland came demands that they be shut down. "CRIME'S SLIMY TRAIL FOLLOWS OPERATIONS OF GAMBLING SHIPS" headlined the September 21, 1933, edition of the *Long Beach Press-Telegram*: "Murder, suspected arson, kidnapping, and other crimes interwoven in a six-year history off Southland Coast."

Officials like Fitts and Hull, who had recognized the ships as a menace since the first appearance off Long Beach, and who had been struggling since 1928 to get rid of them, now found themselves under pressure to do just that from what had heretofore been a largely indifferent and silent majority.

Finally on October 24, 1935, a small article printed in *The Morning Oregonian* said: "Old Steamer *Rose City* Broken Up for Junk." Thus the life of the gambling ship *Johanna Smith II* ex-*Rose Isle* came to an end when her owners sold her to a salvage dealer for ten thousand dollars.

# William H. Harriman
## (1930)

The *William H. Harriman*, a four-masted schooner, was built in 1919, at Thomaston, Maine, to serve as a hauler of coal and other bulk goods. Typical of East Coast schooners, she was a huge vessel—222 feet in length and 43 feet broad in her beam. The post-World War I boom kept the *William H. Harriman* busy carrying cargo to South America and West Africa until 1921. In 1927 R. Cliff Durant of Los Angeles, a sportsman and automobile racer, purchased the vessel and brought her to the Pacific Coast under the command of Captain Paddy Ryan. She sailed through the Panama Canal arriving in the west basin of the Los Angeles harbor on October 4, 1927.

Unfortunately, the California shipping trade was weathering an economic slump at the time. Assignments were hard to come by and shippers were having difficulty keeping their regular carriers busy, let alone newcomers to the docks. Moreover, the labor situation in California ports was highly volatile. Throughout the 1920s, the AFL-based International Longshoremen's Association, headquartered in New York, struggled to gain a foothold on the West Coast trade, controlled at that time by ship employers. Ship employers were fearful of covert infiltration by the International Longshoremen's Association. The former would most likely have been leery of Ryan, a stranger from the East Coast. In any event, Ryan was consistently unsuccessful in his efforts to find work for the *William H. Harriman*, and the ship remained moored in the West Basin. Ryan, his wife, and their daughter lived on board. Occasionally Durant rented her to moving picture companies as a background vessel. When he was no longer interested in the ship, Durant gave her to Ryan.

This state of affairs continued for three years, until, in the summer of 1930, Skipper Ryan met a man by the name of Robinson. Later described by one of the *William H. Harriman*'s crewmen as "a red-headed Englishman, a crook, and a promoter," Robinson expounded to Ryan on the public's love of gambling. Citing the nearby *Johanna Smith* and *Monfalcone* as shining examples, Robinson convinced Ryan that the schooner could make them both rich if used for gambling purposes. The Irish skipper linked up with the English slicker, and they settled on Santa Monica as the place to begin their joint venture.

Ryan arranged to have a powerful deep-sea tug tow the *William H. Harriman* from the Los Angeles harbor some fifteen to twenty miles north. Instead of arriving at the West Basin in late afternoon as scheduled, the tug showed up at 2 A.M. Despite of the pitch-dark waters, the vessels set out, only to run into a fogbank so deeply settled in that no shore lights at all were visible. When Ryan, guided only by the distant sound of cars driving along the coast road, reckoned that his craft had reached a point about a mile out from Santa Monica Pier, he

The schooner *William H. Harriman* was photographed in San Pedro circa 1928.

NOIR AFLOAT

cast off the towline, dropped the bow anchor, and waited for daylight. The tug returned to the Los Angeles harbor.

Daylight and a furious Santa Monica harbormaster arrived together. Fluent in seamen's lingo, the harbormaster favored Ryan with the most abusive terms in his vocabulary as he roared that the schooner was only two hundred yards from the pier and would certainly drift into it, and that the bottom was so sandy a single anchor would never hold her in place. Since no boat powerful enough to tow the *William H. Harriman* was to be found in Santa Monica, a dispirited Ryan dropped a second anchor and sent word for the sea tug to return as soon as possible. It arrived two full days later and pulled the schooner to deeper water, about a mile and one-half from the pier.

Only then did the skipper learn that Robinson had failed to convince Santa Monica officials that they should permit water taxis to use the pier as a departure point for transporting passengers to the ship. As a result, their entire plan fell through. All the towing had been for naught, and the *William H. Harriman* never did operate as a gambling vessel in the vicinity of Santa Monica.

Apparently, Ryan did not lose faith in his new partner, though the latter's ability to make things happen was demonstrably less than he had allowed himself to believe. On August 20, 1930, the *William H. Harriman* dropped anchor farther north, off the shores of Santa Barbara and beyond the three-mile limit. This time, Robinson had exercised foresight by coming to some agreement with that city's water taxis in advance. He also purchased time on the local radio station to advertise the schooner's arrival and pique listeners' interest.

Santa Barbara authorities had no intention of allowing a gambling ship to operate off their coastline. Since the *William H. Harriman* was anchored beyond their jurisdiction, they decided—like Long Beach before them—to aim at the water taxis. They reasoned that if they could prevent people from reaching the gambling ship, lack of business would force her proprietors to move elsewhere.

The taxi operators, meantime, had devised a strategy of sorts. They suddenly became generous in offering "free pleasure jaunts around the harbor." In the course of these, they did not voluntarily mention the schooner. In response to any potential passenger who inquired about the big ship, they insisted they were in no way connected with her. During a pleasure jaunt, however, the taxi would cruise close to the *William H. Harriman*, and its operator would casually offer to pull alongside if anyone wanted to visit her. Almost every passenger did, of course, and was helped aboard and warmly welcomed by the gambling ship's crew.

It is safe to assume, given her size and ample space below decks, to say nothing of her owner's financial straits, that the *William H. Harriman* was neither remodeled nor extensively changed when she assumed her new identity. Hence she retained much of her original beauty, and would have been as interesting an attraction to anyone with an affinity for the sea and ships. Many a coastal resident would have wanted to go aboard her simply to look around. In reporting on her presence, the *Santa Barbara Morning Press* did not even mention her gaming accommodations or the nature or extent of the gambling equipment she carried. It did, however, devote a good deal of attention to related activities of the local police.

On August 24, 1930, peaceful Stearns Wharf at Santa Barbara presented a most unusual sight. Thirty

*William H. Harriman*

**In 1931, Stearns Wharf in Santa Barbara was home to the newly built Santa Barbara Yacht Club. Ramps and stairs led to the floats where passengers boarded water taxis, like the one pictured next to the wharf, and they were off to the *William H. Harriman*.**

police officers armed with clubs confronted some fifteen hundred people waiting for water taxis to take them to the big schooner. Although the majority had come out of curiosity rather than an urge to gamble, police made no attempt to distinguish individuals' motives. They were under orders to prevent anyone from visiting the *William H. Harriman*, and their determination to follow those orders resulted in a spontaneous Keystone comedy.

Near the wharf was a breakwater, extending from the beach out to sea, with a wide path for strollers running along its top. As police blocked prospective water taxi passengers from entering boarding docks on the wharf, the taxis moved to the end of the breakwater. So did the people, who began boarding them there. Irate police rushed to the breakwater, whereupon both taxis and people returned to the wharf. The crowd, choosing to be amused, was soon making a game of it all. Some adventurous souls even commandeered whatever rowboats they could find and propelled themselves into the harbor waters, where they transferred to the cooperative taxis.

A powerful seagoing tug towed the *William H. Harriman* from one location to another. The schooner is shown here shortly before her gambling-ship days, because the landing platform is not yet attached to her side.

Finally conceding the benefit of the doubt to those who insisted they only wanted to take the harbor cruise and had no wish to board the schooner, the police—by that time run ragged—allowed them to board taxis. However, they counted the number of passengers departing in each boat, announcing that if the same number did not debark when it returned, they would confiscate the taxi. Returning taxi operators who had lost passengers to the *William H. Harriman* defeated that stratagem by claiming they had dropped the missing ones off at the breakwater on their way in.

Increasing the pressure, police declared that any person going to the gambling ship would be arrested on charges of "attempting to commit a crime," and further intimidated those still waiting for taxis by pointing out that whoever insisted on boarding the schooner would do so at the risk of being stranded on her once the taxis were forced to stopped running. The pandemonium came to an abrupt halt when police actually arrested

The four-masted schooner *William H. Harriman*, on the right, tied up with other idle ships at Terminal Island. With her landing platform still attached, she is waiting to be scuttled.

NOIR AFLOAT

a man demanding to board one of the taxis and charged him with disturbing the peace. People didn't feel like playing anymore, the taxis ceased trying to operate, and the crowd slowly dispersed. Asked about earlier passengers now marooned on the ship, a police spokesman declared: "Too bad if they lied and went aboard. It's their own fault, and they can find a way back any way they can!" Around midnight, however, the police relented and sent a boat out to fetch them home.

Ryan and Robinson, their plans at least temporarily thwarted, decided to have the *William H. Harriman* towed a short distance south to Ventura, where the Loyal Order of Moose was holding a three-day state convention. Robinson was sure so many conventioneers would prove a fine source of patronage. Ventura officials, on the other hand, were not in the least pleased when the schooner came into view of their city.

When the *William H. Harriman* opened to accommodate the conventioneers, they ferried would-be customers to her from the nearby and private Pierpont Bay Pier, whose owners, out of town at the time, had no idea their property was being trespassed upon. Although the big schooner did a thriving business the first night, repeat customers were lacking the next. Either the members of the Moose simply didn't enjoy gambling, or they had returned to shore with empty pockets—cleaned out in one evening. A disconsolate Ryan once more ordered a tug, and within a few days the *William H. Harriman* was hauled south again. Ryan anchored her off Long Beach, where she lay for over a month, doing no business to speak of and enduring one threat after another from the operators of the *Johanna Smith*. Eventually, he gave up and had her towed into the Los Angeles harbor. She languished there for the next ten years.

The schooner's end came in late 1940 during a severe storm. A neighboring 360-foot Romanian steamer, named *Prahova*, dragged her anchor and drifted into the once impressive four-master with enough force to cripple her. At the time of the collision, Skipper Ryan was still vainly seeking contracts for her. But the extensive damage to her bow, combined with her rotting timbers, proved more than he could deal with. He formally abandoned the twenty-one-year-old ship. Taken over by the Coast Guard, the *William H. Harriman* was tied up at Terminal Island along with other old vessels, where, as the months passed, she gradually settled into the mud and her deteriorating timbers continued to weaken. On July 21, 1941, her bilge was pumped out, pontoons were attached to her hull, and she was re-floated. The cost of repairing her was estimated at $125,000, and her sailing days were declared over. Subsequently, the War Department contracted for her disposal. She was loaded with seven hundred tons of rock and towed to a point four miles south of Point Fermin, where two loads of dynamite were set off in her hold and she slowly sank to her final resting place sixty fathoms deep.

*William H. Harriman*

163

GUEST CARD

*The Play Yacht* CASINO

cordially invites

Mr...........................................and party
to be their guests for Dinner Dancing and Entertainment
any convenient evening.
Free Insided Parking

THIS GUEST CARD DEFRAYS ALL DINNER AND DANCING EXPENSE

**The beautiful four-masted barkentine *James Tuft* is photographed under sail with a deck load of lumber.**

NOIR AFLOAT

# Casino ex-*James Tuft*
## (1935)

For anyone who loves ships, the story of the *Casino ex-James Tuft* is a sad tale. Built in 1901, she was a beautiful four-masted barkentine made from yellow fir wood. She was constructed by the Hall Brothers firm in Port Blakely, Washington. The cost of her construction was $74,000. By far the largest of her kind, she weighed 1,274 tons and had a carrying capacity of 1,400,000 board feet of lumber. For twenty-eight years, she was a beautiful sight to see as she sailed up and down the Pacific Coast between Puget Sound and Southern California waters, carrying fine Northwest timber to waiting Southwest home builders.

In 1928, she was retired from service and sold to Claude Cummings, for use as a fishing barge. Cummings initially anchored her at Redondo Beach, but by 1932 he had moved her north to Venice, anchoring her somewhat less than three miles off the Venice Pier, and continuing to operate her solely as a fishing barge. Before that year was out, though, the once proud ship was being used twice a month for "Stag Shows," whose attractions included exhibitions of indecent dancing, a carnival of drinking and gambling, lewd sexual acts, prostitutes, etc.

Prohibition was still in force, and on the night of December 18, 1932, fifteen of the three hundred men who boarded the *James Tuft* to engage in such "spicy and unconventional high jinks on the high seas" were police in plain clothes, masquerading as participants while no fewer than sixty uniformed police and federal agents aboard the U.S. Coast Guard cutter *Ewing* sped to join them. According to the next day's *Los Angeles Examiner*:

> The raid was one of the most spectacular and dangerous ever undertaken by authorities in Southern California waters. Blinding "pea-soup" fog hampered operations, and heavy ground swells crashed the cutter again and again against the towering four-master as Guardsmen tried to pass mooring lines over her rails. Meantime, the plainclothesmen on board, their identity discovered, were fighting for their lives, while operators of the vessel dumped quantities of liquor overboard.

Once the armed police and federal raiding squads managed to get onto the fog-shrouded deck and down into the ship's creaking and crowded hold, they put a stop to the pandemonium. Then, surrounded on all sides with evidence—a bar (still stocked with an ample supply of beer), gaming tables, roulette wheels, slot machines, a rumba band, and scantily clad performers of both sexes—they arrested nineteen men and four women on various charges, including violation of the Volstead Act and state liquor and gambling laws, participation

*Casino ex-James Tuft*

NOIR AFLOAT

in lewd and indecent exhibitions, and even possession of obscene photographs. After sending their prisoners back to shore in speedboats to be held at the Venice Police Station, they released the spectators.

In those days, it was customary for the newspapers to list the names and addresses of people arrested. Cummings was not among those rounded up on the *James Tuft*, and the extent to which he was involved in defiling the good ship *James Tuft* remains unknown. In any event, he took her back to Redondo Beach, where she enjoyed a slightly more respectable status as a fishing barge for two more years. Nor do the records show whether her ownership changed hands when she was later converted to a gambling ship, renamed the *Casino*, and towed to gambling ship row.

The *Casino* was not destined to remain in her new role for long. Three weeks after her opening, a leak developed in her forward hold that proved difficult for her pumps to handle. Although this was not an uncommon occurrence in a wooden vessel of her age, the situation was serious enough to render her unsafe if a large crowd was aboard. Her owner or owners closed her down, leaving three caretakers to guard her and tend to the pumps, until such time as they could take her to a repair dock. For whatever reason, they never got around to doing so, and the weary old barkentine lay idle offshore all through that spring and summer.

At six o'clock on the evening of August 22, 1935, one of the *Casino's* caretakers, following his usual routine, went below to start the gasoline engine of the generator that supplied her electricity. Unaware that gasoline fumes had been gathering in the engine room, he pushed the starter. The resulting explosion set the entire room ablaze with flames that quickly spread toward the ship's gasoline and oil stores and hurled the caretaker, clothes aflame, to the bottom of a companionway. Rushing to his rescue, his fellow workers struggled to get him on deck, themselves becoming human torches in the process. All three leaped overboard. The nearby *Monte Carlo* had already launched a boat, which picked them up minutes later. Taken aboard that ship, they were then transferred to a water taxi that sped them to land, where an ambulance rushed them to Long Beach's Seaside Hospital.

For the third time, crowds of spectators gathered along the coast to watch the fiery demise of a gambling ship. The *Casino* ex-*James Tuft* burned with such intense heat that within an hour she was consumed to the water line. Coast Guard boats standing by could do nothing to save her. Jets of flame and billowing clouds of black smoke were visible from all the neighboring beach cities. The three young caretakers—two of them only in their early twenties—were reported in the next morning's papers as suffering from second- and third-degree burns on their faces and bodies, but not in critical condition. The pain, trauma, and scarring that lay ahead for them were left to readers' imaginations.

On August 24, Coast Guardsmen towed the charred remains of the once superb sailing ship to breaking-up docks, where sledges and saws could complete her devastation. Her career as a floating casino ended before it really began, and her story is included here primarily in tribute to her original splendor.

The gambling ship *Casino*, formerly the *James Tuft*, caught fire in 1935 and burned to the water line. The remains were towed ashore and cut into scrap.

*Casino ex-James Tuft*

# Monte Carlo
## (1932-1936)

The *Monte Carlo* was built in 1921 at Wilmington, North Carolina, as part of a government-sponsored experiment in constructing ships from alternative materials. A tanker whose hull was made entirely of concrete, she proved so much heavier than steel and wooden-hulled craft that her builders felt free to delete concrete from their list of practicable choices. Nevertheless, she was a usable vessel and served two years in the U.S. Quartermaster Corps with the name *Tanker No.1*. In 1923, the Associated Oil Company of San Francisco acquired the vessel and renamed her *McKittrick*. She worked for the company from then on as an oil tanker along the Pacific Coast for almost a decade.

In 1932 she was sold and converted into a gambling ship at Wilmington, California. The *Monte Carlo* ex-*McKittrick* was towed out to sea and anchored near the *Johanna Smith*. She was a good size vessel, three hundred feet in length with a forty-four-foot beam. She was bigger than her neighbor and all other gambling ships

**Associated Oil Company built its tanker *McKittrick* in 1921.**

**The *Monte Carlo* was called the world's largest pleasure ship and considered the best of the gambling ships in its day.**

that preceded her. The proud owners of this vessel were Ed V. Turner and Marvin "Doc" Schouweiler, who was previously a part owner of the *Johanna Smith*.

Her owners were anticipating with pleasure the upcoming August opening at Los Angeles of the 1932 Olympic Games. Long Beach was the venue chosen for the rowing races, and that attraction, as well as all the other Olympic events, gave promise of a tremendous influx of visitors to the area, crowds of whom would undoubtedly make their way to gambling ship row.

In thousands of announcements both mailed and hand-distributed, the *Monte Carlo*'s owners promoted her May 7, 1932, grand opening. They described her as "the world's greatest pleasure ship" reachable by water taxis leaving at fifteen-minute intervals from the dock at 1375 West Seventh Street, Long Beach. They had by

*Monte Carlo*

These **DICE ARE 100% PERFECT**
**THEY ARE FREE**
ASK THE DEALER FOR A PAIR

NOIR NFLONT

this time added banquet service to their list of attractions and were openly soliciting luncheon or dinner party business from social or professional clubs, office staffs, and other organizational groups. That same summer, the *Long Beach Morning Sun* riveted its readers' attention with a series of twelve daily articles, exposing every facet of the gambling ships' operations.

The reporter had been given access to all the records police had seized in their raids on the docks, and he put them to use in calculating just how much money was involved in the operation of the *Johanna Smith*, the *Rose Isle*, and the *Monte Carlo* during the summer of 1932. Checkers at the water taxi bases kept careful record of the number of people going out to the ships each day, and from these the reporter determined that between Saturday noon and 2 A.M. Sunday morning on the weekend of July 9, a total of 4,486 patrons visited the floating casinos. Of these, 1,240 went to the *Rose Isle*, 1,510 to the *Johanna Smith*, and 1,736 to the newly opened *Monte Carlo*.

On the basis of a statement made by one of the ships' owners and verified by "those in the know," every customer could be counted upon to leave a ship with at least five dollars less than he or she had brought aboard. Thus, based on an obviously conservative figure of five dollars per head, the income to the three ships that weekend was $6,250 for the *Rose Isle*, $7,550 for the *Johanna Smith*, and $8,680 for the *Monte Carlo*. Reliable sources had estimated the cost per day of operating any one of the vessels at approximately one thousand dollars, hence with the cash intake above, all the ships had covered an entire week's expenses in just fourteen hours.

Enlarging the picture, a total of fifteen thousand people a week boarded one or another of the ships, leaving $75,000 behind when they headed back to shore. Subtracting their combined weekly operating costs of $21,000 from that figure showed that the syndicates were netting $54,000 a week—or $2,808,000 a year from their floating casinos.

On March 15, 1934, Long Beach Chief McClelland and a squad of eight policemen, dressed in plain clothes and posing as customers, infiltrated three outgoing water taxis. When the boats reached the *Monte Carlo*, they lingered aboard them until the unsuspecting passengers had all been helped onto the gambling ship. Then, revealing their identity, they forced the taxi operators to return to land. Upon the taxi's return to the dock, authorities arrested the six men who had manned the taxis and two others in charge of operations at the

**The *Monte Carlo* featured a huge gambling casino. *Above:* The casino is photographed toward the stern of the ship. *Opposite:* this view looks toward the bow.**

*Monte Carlo*

171

shore end. All eight were booked at the Long Beach police station on suspicion of violating "the state law which prohibits taking persons to a gambling ship whether it be in or out of the State of California". There was no more taxi service that night, and nearly four hundred thoroughly angered patrons were stranded for hours aboard the *Monte Carlo* until arrangements were made to bring them ashore.

Two months later, on May 3, 1934, as the sun sank below the Southern California horizon, the twinkling lights of the *Monte Carlo* came to life. Trimly dressed crew members took their places on her landing platform, ready to pull early bird patrons safely on board and help them up the narrow ladder to the deck. From that point on other crew members would direct them to the spacious and elegant dining and dancing salon, the hospitable taproom with its amazingly long and highly polished bar and myriad tempting alcoholic beverages, and the immense and softly lit casino—furnished from one end to the other with exciting and diverting games for them to play.

By 10 P.M. the evening was in full swing. Some five hundred patrons were living it up, most of them in the game room, as two new arrivals came aboard. One of them seized a microphone. Upon hearing his voice the room fell silent. Los Angeles District Attorney Buron Fitts introduced himself and his companion, Orange County District Attorney S.B. Kauffman. He then announced that the *Monte Carlo* was now in their custody. Simultaneously, fifteen undercover agents revealed their identity and rounded up the eight taxi operators waiting to begin that night's return trips. Herding them into a group, the agents arrested all eight on the spot, thus preventing anyone from leaving the ship.

From stunned silence, the crowd burst into pandemonium. Unaware of the arrests already made, hysterical passengers rushed to the ship's rails shouting for taxis to take them ashore. Assurances from the agents that

**The ship's giant bar featured just about any kind of liquor one could desire.**

patrons would not be arrested eventually quieted them down. Meanwhile, agents arrested owners Ed V. Turner, "Doc" Schouweiler, and eight dealers. Together with the eight taximen, they were transported to Los Angeles County Jail, booked on a blanket charge of conspiracy to violate California gambling laws, and held there until their arraignment the next day.

For the first time, Los Angeles and Orange Counties had worked together to thwart the gambling syndicate. Fitts and Kauffman had caught the *Monte Carlo's* owners and operators completely by surprise. Both those facts were so exciting that not one report bothered to mention how the five hundred patrons aboard the ship that night ever managed to get home.

Fitts and Kauffman had decided that Los Angeles County would prosecute the entire body of men arrested in the previous night's raid, the owners, dealers, and taximen, while Orange County would prosecute only the owners and dealers. Determined to present the strongest possible case, Kauffman and his men now returned by daylight to the *Monte Carlo* and stripped her of every bit of her gambling equipment.

The evidence collected included seven dice tables, seven blackjack tables, eight roulette tables and wheels, her complete chuck-a-luck and Chinese lottery paraphernalia, stacks and stacks of cards and chips, innumerable sets of dice, and no fewer than twenty-seven slot machines still filled with cash. Attendants on board tried to retrieve the coins from the slots, but the operation was moving too quickly. Otherwise, there was no resistance, as furniture and furnishings were methodically hauled on deck and lowered into waiting tugboats. It was reported that the ship's orchestra played "Farewell to Thee", as load after load of material disappeared over the side.

Meanwhile, the eighteen men under arrest were arraigned in Los Angeles Municipal Court

**The dining room was elegant with linen tablecloths and crystal. A small dance floor and orchestra entertained.**

*Monte Carlo*

**Racks holding silver dollars were kept in the counting room; note the gun.**

on a blanket misdemeanor charge of conspiracy to violate California gambling laws, and given until May 14 to plead. Bail was set, after which the two owners and eight operators among them were transported to Orange County for arraignment on charges of gambling, a violation of section 330 of the state penal code, and placed under additional bail. As soon as that evening, all eighteen defendants were free on bail. Their attorneys indicated that they would base their defense on the everlastingly employable grounds of lack of jurisdiction.

The May 3, 1934, raid of the *Monte Carlo* was the most impressive assault to date on any tenant of gambling ship row. Indeed, factoring into the attack Orange District Attorney Kauffman's subsequent seizure of the vessel's gaming equipment, as well as Los Angeles District Attorney Fitts's warning to the public that in future anyone found patronizing a floating casino would be liable to arrest, it appeared that local law enforcement officials might finally have cooked the gamblers' golden goose. Such was not the case. In the ongoing war between civil authorities and gambling profiteers, the advantage had merely shifted from one side to the other. Within a week, the see-saw syndrome that had characterized the contest from its start emerged once more.

Having accomplished the relatively simple task of getting eighteen men released on bail by both Los Angeles and Orange County courts, attorneys for the defense moved next to put them back in business. This time, however, they divided their efforts. On May 8, attorney Jonah Jones, Jr., convinced a Los Angeles Superior Court judge to issue a temporary restraining order against any interference by agents of the district attorney or the police with the activities of water taxis plying between Long Beach and the *Monte Carlo*, pending the result of the upcoming Orange County trial.

Meanwhile, in Orange County, attorney Jonah Jones, Sr., went after the confiscated gambling equipment. The Justice of Seal Beach, accepting Jones's declaration that the *Monte Carlo* lay outside state jurisdiction, ordered the county sheriff to return all gambling paraphernalia to the ship's owners. Apprised of this maneuver, an outraged Kauffman promptly sought a temporary injunction from Orange Superior Court against the sheriff taking any such action. The necessary hearing took place on May 10.

**Gamblers tried their luck at the Wheel of Fortune, a special favorite of the ladies.**

Turner, Schouweiler, and the eight dealers from the *Monte Carlo* appeared for trial in the Seal Beach Court of Justice. They stood trial before a local jury of nine men and three women, with Justice Fred Smith presiding. Defense attorneys freely admitted their clients had been engaged in running a place of gambling at the time of their arrest. Given the evidence the prosecution displayed, they could hardly state otherwise. They argued, of course, that since the activities in question took place outside the state and on the high seas, no court in the state had jurisdiction in the matter. To prove their argument, they deluged the court with maps from numerous sources. They brought up and left unanswered the question of whether the courts, the federal authorities, or even mapmakers in general were empowered to set the confines of a bay, and drew numerous giggles and guffaws from the jury with their humorous remarks.

For its part, the jury ignored the evidence presented by the prosecution, including the earlier ruling of Judge Ames that the *Monte Carlo's* location was clearly within the jurisdiction of the township, the county, and the state. It also ignored Seal Beach Justice Smith's instruction that if the ship was at the spot designated on the maps presented by the prosecutors, then it was indeed within the Justice Court's jurisdiction. After deliberating for less than two hours, the jury produced a blanket acquittal. Accordingly, Justice Smith exonerated all ten defendants, and noted that the *Monte Carlo's* equipment should be returned to her owners.

In 1935, the *Monte Carlo* closed down for the night after a busy Fourth of July weekend. Nobody heard

*Monte Carlo*

NOIR AFLOAT

On May 3, 1934, Los Angeles and Orange County authorities raided the *Monte Carlo*, closing the ship. They stripped the ship of its gambling equipment, including tables and chairs; everything was taken ashore as evidence and stored in a warehouse. However, the judge ruled the officials did not have the authority to take the equipment, so they were forced to return it to the ship.

*Monte Carlo*

**Pirates stole the fishing boat *Nolla* and used it to reach the *Monte Carlo*.**

the muffled sounds of a fishing boat pulling up alongside the vessel. It was 3:30 in the morning. Four masked men appeared in the salon armed with guns and chains. They used the chains to tie hostages to bar stools. They worked silently to avoid waking up the crew members sleeping below. They went to the bookkeepers' cabin and demanded that the door be opened. When the pirates left, they took with them $22,000 in silver and currency and $10,000 worth of watches and jewelry. (The watches and jewelry were being held as collateral for advances made to patrons who were out of money.) They returned to the fishing boat and chugged away to meet a waiting speedboat. They chopped a hole in the bottom of the fishing boat, thinking it would sink. Then they sped back to the Los Angeles harbor, where they tied up the speedboat and went to the nearby home of one of the pirates and divided up the loot.

A fisherman heading out to sea in the early morning spotted the fishing boat wallowing in the water. He towed it to the *Monte Carlo* and left it there. The police managed to track down its owner, who explained that it had been stolen from its mooring place. He also informed the police about two men that showed up at his place offering to buy the boat. He let them take it for a test ride. During the test ride, the men had apparently duplicated the boat's keys.

Undercover police were staked out in a bar on the waterfront. In came a man they knew as a drifter with no job and no money. He ordered drinks at the bar and gave the waitress a five-dollar tip. He also handed five dollars to the prostitutes who were gathered there, too. The police arrested him and took him to the police station, where they questioned him about flashing money and about the nice suit of clothes he was wearing. The prisoner broke down and confessed that he was a member of the mob that robbed the gambling ship.

He told a sad story about how he was in a bar complaining about being broke and unemployed. He said a companion told him he knew somebody who needed a person for a one-time job. The companion wrote down a telephone number on a piece of paper and said to call him. The next day, he called and was told to be at the corner of Seventh and Alvarado Streets, in Los Angeles, and he would be picked up. A man in a blue Buick picked him up, and they drove to Wilmington where they met two other men. They picked up guns, loaded them into the car, and headed for the harbor. From there they boarded a speedboat and headed out to sea. They stopped at a certain point and waited. Soon a small fishing boat came alongside. All the men put black hoods over their heads with holes cut out for their eyes. They put black socks over their shoes and got into the fishing boat, then headed for the *Monte Carlo*. They waited until 3:30 in the morning when the lights on the ship went off. They went to the loading platform and slowly climbed aboard.

From the descriptions given, the police caught the perpetrators and arrested them. The leaders of the gang were the proprietors of a beer joint in Wilmington called the Owl. They were sent to a federal prison for eight years.

In 1936, ostensibly to get away from the constant harassment of Long Beach and Los Angeles authorities, the owners of the *Monte Carlo* decided to try San Diego for a change. San Diego, located about 120 miles south of Los Angeles, was then a navy town. In the 1930s the *Monte Carlo* could have anticipated a supply of customers—not only from the navy, but from civilians on land in a town that had a more tolerant attitude toward gambling than L.A. and Long Beach. Still, officials there were searching for a way to rid San Diego of the gambling ship, but were unsuccessful.

After hosting a gala party on November 1, 1936, the *Monte Carlo* closed for the winter. On board were stationed two caretakers to keep an eye on things until the following spring. On December 30, Southern California's weather turned bad. Snow fell in the mountains, unrelenting rains turned hillsides into mudslides, gale-force winds toppled trees, and small-craft warnings went up all along the entire Southland coast. Around the big *Monte Carlo* the sea churned and heaved. Waves twelve feet high pounded her hull. Around 3:30 A.M. the morning of New Year's Eve, the *Monte Carlo*'s anchor chains, stressed to the breaking point by the power of the storm, snapped. She began to drift helplessly. Her caretakers stranded aboard were terrified. They sent up distress flares one after the other but nobody saw them. By morning the vessel had drifted shoreward and ended up hard aground on the Coronado Strand.

The big Coast Guard vessel *Itasca* came to attempt a rescue of the men trapped aboard. Though the rain had ceased, the ocean raged with towering waves and the gale-force winds continued. The Coast Guard vessel launched a small powerboat with five men to attempt to maneuver alongside the wreck. The formidable waves were still pounding against the gambling ship's hull. One by one, the caretakers managed to creep down on a Jacob's ladder, then leap into the Guardsman's launch. The men could only let go and jump into the craft at the crest of a wave before it plunged down into a watery trough. Once both the men successfully negotiated the nightmare leap and were wrapped in warm blankets, the powerboat battled its way back to the *Itasca*.

Powerful waves continued to pound the *Monte Carlo*. Eventually the wooden deckhouse that housed the gambling casino broke apart and washed ashore. Along with it came furniture and gambling equipment. The crowd that gathered to see the stranded gambling ship collected flotsam as souvenirs until the police put a halt to that. More and more people came to stand on the beach and watch the *Monte Carlo* break apart.

Suddenly the crowd gasped in horror when a young man plunged into the sea and swam to the stranded vessel. While attempting to climb the anchor chain, a huge wave washed him off and carried him away. His body was never found.

None of the owners of the *Monte Carlo* ever came to claim the wreck. They just walked away and left her on the beach. The concrete hull had broken in half, making it impossible to float her away. She slowly sank into the sand and was eventually buried, leaving only memories of an amazing history of offshore gambling.

*Monte Carlo*

Anchored in San Diego on New Year's Day in 1936, the *Monte Carlo* was caught in a violent storm. Her anchor chains broke and the big ship, with only her watchmen aboard, drifted toward the shore. The pounding sea battered the ship, which had become stuck in the sand, and soon its gambling equipment began washing ashore.

NOIR NFLONT

When the New Year's Day storm finally ended, the *Monte Carlo* was totally wrecked. The casino was gone, the concrete hull was firmly stuck in the sand and the hull was broken in half, making it impossible to float. The sorry wreck remained stranded and eventually sank, buried in the sand where she remains to this day.

*Monte Carlo*

# Caliente, Sho-Boat, Mount Baker
## (1937-1938)

The *Mount Shasta* was built in Portland, Oregon in 1918. She was a 285-foot-long wooden freighter designed to haul large loads. She saw service in World War I, at which time she was renamed *Mount Baker*. She retained that name when she entered the salmon fishing business in 1923.

In 1937, the Red Salmon Fishing Company of San Francisco sold the *Mount Baker* to a man by the name of Marion Hicks. Hicks identified himself as vice president of the Atlas Finance Corporation located in Los Angeles. In actuality, Hicks was the front man for a syndicate of which he may or may not have been a partner. Later events would reveal that the Atlas Finance Corporation was non-existent, and that the address he gave for the company was that of a Plymouth auto dealership where he had at one time worked as a salesman.

After purchasing the *Mount Baker*, Hicks registered her in San Francisco and had her towed south for conversion to a gambling ship. He named her *Caliente*. By mid-summer 1937, the *Caliente* was ready for her casino career. Her gaming area was large enough to include practically every form of gambling device, and she boasted the usual ancillary amenities—dining salon, dance floor, cocktail lounge and buffet, etc. Reportedly, her furnishings alone had cost one hundred thousand dollars, and she would be stocked at any given time with at least five thousand dollars worth of food and liquor. Towed out to sea at the end of June, she dropped anchor in the vicinity of the *Tango*, and began receiving customers by way of the Deluxe Water Taxi Company, whose boats operated from the P & O dock at 501 Pico Boulevard.

The *Caliente* operated for more than a year without generating a newsworthy event. This ended in September 1938, when a man was found dead on her upper deck with a bullet hole in his temple. Long Beach police termed it a suicide. However, the gruesome discovery gave rise to a spate of bad publicity. In an attempt to cool things down, the *Caliente*'s owners changed her name to *Sho-Boat*. It is hard to believe such a ploy had anything to do with the fact that she continued to prosper.

In February 1939, for the usual purpose of concealing their individual identities, the owners of the *Sho-Boat* had the United States Corporation Company in Nevada set up a company called the Mount Baker

**FOLLOW THESE EASY DIRECTIONS**
**TO THRILL and EXCITEMENT!**

Just drive to the corner of Pico and 5th Streets in Long Beach . . . Then the huge electric sign, pictured below, will direct you to fun and pleasure aboard the CALIENTE.

S.S.
CALIENTE
PO DOCK
501 PICO ENTRANCE

**SPEEDBOATS**
Leave Every 15 Minutes
**25c ROUND TRIP**
**FREE PARKING**

**The gambling ship known as *Caliente*, *Sho-Boat* and *Mount Baker*, anchored off Long Beach.**

Amusement Company. The dummy corporation would be listed as the owner of the ship instead of the Atlas Finance Company, actually Marion Hicks. The Mount Baker Amusement Corporation bought the ship with a $86,100 loan and the ship as collateral. They changed the ship's name back to its original name – the *Mount Baker*. She continued to operate for the rest of the year—sometimes off Long Beach and sometimes off Venice.

Ironically, the Nevada caper did not serve to conceal the identity of the ship's owners from the Long Beach police. The latter had known who they were since her arrival on the row, if not before. In addition to Hicks, the syndicate consisted of Martin Schultheis, a realtor who had lived in Long Beach for years; Hayden C. Smith and Arthur Benson, who jointly ran a pool hall in Long Beach, with gambling rooms and bookmaking facilities in the rear; George G. Parry and Ballard Barron, operators of a café in adjacent Seal Beach with a similar backroom set up; and, last but not least, William Gleason, whose partnership in the *Rose Isle* and subsequent

*Caliente, Sho-Boat, Mount Baker*

management of the *Johanna Smith II* constituted only two of his numerous ship and shore gambling interests in Southern California. All local boys, you might say.

On August 1, 1938, during Warren's massive raid of four gambling ships that would end the gambling ship era, the *Mount Baker* was located off Long Beach near the *Tango*. During the raid, Warren Olney and Burdette Daniels had not found the *Mount Baker* quite as cooperative as the *Tango*. They managed to confiscate her bankroll and shut her down, but her operators refused to move her out of her Long Beach location or allow her gambling equipment to be seized. The officials returned her bankroll and let her alone for the time being. Then, on December 28, 1939, Oscar Jahnsen, representing the attorney general; Fred Hender-

**Tickets for a complimentary dinner aboard the *Caliente* were a come-on to gamblers.** *Left:* **The sign at 501 Pico Avenue in Long Beach points to the water taxi dock.**

son, representing District Attorney Fitts; and Tommy Wishon, a Long Beach police officer, boarded the Fish and Game boat *Tuna* and, armed with a Superior Court order, headed out to the ship to seize the equipment. The *Mount Baker* must have been alerted to what was coming because the *Tuna* found her about eight miles out to sea and under tow by the tug *Plover*.

The officers ordered the tug to cut the towline and then pulled alongside the ship. The *Mount Baker's* crew began spraying the officers with high-pressure water hoses as ship manager Marion Hicks exclaimed, "I am the manager and we are on the high seas and you have no authority."

Backing off for that day, the *Tuna* and her occupants tried again the next day. This time, Jahnsen resorted to trickery. The *Mount Baker's* captain, Hans Anderson, instead of immediately repeating the previous day's water attack, shouted out, "You can't come aboard!" "We've got a warrant," Jahnsen yelled back. "Let's see who signed it," shouted Anderson, lowering a rope to which Jahnsen could attach it. Jahnsen complied. Anderson pulled the rope back up and was unfolding the warrant when Jahnsen called to him: "You have accepted service of a warrant, and we're coming up." Suiting his action to his words, Jahnsen started up the ship's ladder. A blast of water from the high-pressure hose hit him immediately, soaking him to the skin. At that, the other officials on the *Tuna* drew their guns. The crew aboard the *Mount Baker* surrendered at the sight, and the authorities climbed aboard.

They confiscated forty thousand dollars worth of gambling equipment, including one hundred slot machines, seven roulette wheels, five blackjack tables, a wheel of fortune, two chuck-a-luck, and two poker tables, all of which went to a warehouse. Judge Emmet Wilson issued a preliminary injunction and a show cause order, returnable January 5, at which the owners could present their argument as to why the attorney general's office should be prevented from destroying the paraphernalia.

In the meantime, another preliminary injunction prevented the *Mount Baker* from moving to a different location or anchorage. This legal action had been taken against the Mount Baker Amusement Company of Nevada by the Atlas Finance Company. To keep the authorities from confiscating the ship, Atlas Finance

A water taxi at the dock waits for passengers before it speeds to the *Caliente*.

*Caliente, Sho-Boat, Mount Baker*

claimed it was holding a promissory note in the amount of $86,100, for which the Mount Baker Amusement Company had posted the *Mount Baker* as collateral. Atlas maintained the vessel was still seaworthy and, with a few alterations, could ply in coastwise or foreign trade. To satisfy the lien, the United States marshal sold the ship and the Atlas Finance Company got its $86,100.

The ship was sold to an Edward H. Lacey in 1940. He in turn sold the ship to P.F. Soto of Los Angeles in 1941. Soto owned a large shipping business and completely reconditioned the ship for cargo use. In December of 1942, Soto sold her to the War Shipping Administration, and the ship went to Alaska to serve in the U.S. Army as an ammunition ship. During World War II, the army operated a fleet of general utility vessels that could serve

The *Caliente* featured a sophisticated casino.

NOIR AFLOAT

as freighters and passenger vessels. This operation was secondary to that of the navy and served those areas where command responsibilities had been assigned to the army. The *Mount Baker* served in that capacity in Alaska. She was one of only a few of the World War I wooden hulled freighters which survived for twenty-three years and was still serviceable by the time World War II shipping needs increased.

Near the end of World War II, on February 26, 1944, at Prince Rupert, British Columbia, she caught fire. The wooden vessel burned to the waterline while transiting the Inside Passage to Alaska. She was beached at Prince Rupert, British Columbia. One report said she became part of the breakwater being constructed at that time.

**Officers tried to serve a warrant to seize the gambling ship equipment still on board the *Mount Baker*. They failed the first day, but served the warrant the next day, went aboard and removed the equipment, took it ashore and stored it in a warehouse.
*Above right:* For a short period, the name of the ship had been changed to *Sho-Boat*. In 1939, the name was changed again, this time to her original name, *Mount Baker*.**

*Caliente, Sho-Boat, Mount Baker*

# Cruises to Nowhere

The H.M.S. *Mistletoe* was no stranger to adventure, intrigue or excitement. She started her career as a member of the Royal Navy. She had been built in 1918 for use by the British navy in World War I. She served a little over three years as a "Q" ship. She was camouflaged from the rudder to masthead to look like a slow freighter, but was actually a fast cruiser equipped with powerful batteries capable of blowing a submarine out of the water.

Sometime in 1922, the H.M.S *Mistletoe* was sold, along with other ships of her kind, to a Mexican shipping company. She was registered in Mazatlan and renamed *Chiapas*. She then operated as a freighter between San Francisco and Central America.

**Hotel and casino Playa Ensenada was on the edge of the sea, about eighteen miles south of the border. When gambling was outlawed in Mexico in 1935, it suffered a drastic decline in business.**

NOIR AFLOAT

The ship *La Playa*, eager to bring customers to Mexico, came to the Los Angeles harbor. The huge ship depicted on the brochure bears no resemblance to the real ship.

By 1932, gambling casinos had begun to flourish in Baja California, Mexico, many of them backed by American investors and run by American gamblers. Tijuana's multi-million-dollar Agua Caliente, with its first-class hotel, elegant casino, and on-site racetrack, had become an international attraction. Further to the south, in the little port city of Ensenada, was another beautiful gambling resort, La Playa Ensenada, one of whose major financial backers was Jack Dempsey, the world-champion boxer.

Because of its location on the ocean, close to the harbor, the management of La Playa Ensenada planned to offer its U.S. customers round-trip service by water from San Diego. They purchased the *Chiapas* for this purpose, and changed her name to *Playa Ensenada*. She completed only a single round trip from San Diego before U.S. navigation laws interfered with the plan.

She was sold to new owners in 1933, who abbreviated her name to *La Playa* and moved her to San Pedro, California, to inaugurate an unusual trip called "Cruises to Nowhere" from Pier 60 in the outer harbor. When the following enticing advertisement appeared in the newspapers, sizable numbers of Southern California thrill-seekers were quick to respond:

Six Golden Hours on the High Seas

Here is a trip you will enjoy. Six golden hours of carefree pleasure on the high seas. An evening filled with an amazing variety of vivacious amusement, thrilling pleasure, and delightful entertainment. Dining. Dancing. Tempting Refreshments. Sportive Games. A stimulating ocean voyage. A hilarious holiday where revelry reigns supreme. An evening such as would delight your fancy in gay Havana or on the famed French Riviera, at Nice, Cannes, Monte Carlo or Juan les Pins.

The "Sportive Games" were gambling and those "Tempting Refreshments" were booze. *La Playa* was under Panamanian registry so it could carry liquor. When she pulled into any American port, U.S. customs sealed the storage compartments holding all kinds of hard liquor, beer, and wine, as well as gallons of pure alcohol from which new concoctions could be created. But once on the high seas, beyond U.S. jurisdiction, the

liquor cabinets were opened and her games of chance got under way. Since Prohibition was still in effect at this time, the "Cruises to Nowhere" were an instant success.

On the evening of March 10, 1932, some one hundred patrons planning to take the cruise found uniformed harbor guards blocking the gangway leading to the ship. The guards informed them that if they boarded her, they would not be permitted to disembark at the dock. Apparently the operators of the ship had failed to acquire the proper permits from the Harbor Department to use the harbor facilities. Nine days later, the mayor of Los Angeles and the Harbor Commission president jointly announced that neither the *La Playa* nor any other gambling ships would be permitted to operate from municipally owned docks ever again. The owners gave up, sold the ship, discharged the ship's crew without pay, and faced the wrath of the twenty-eight crew members who filed suit in federal court for recovery of back wages.

In 1933, *La Playa* was purchased by Martin S. Lewis, Jr., who kept her under Panamanian registry and changed her name to *City of Panama*. He leased the ship to Clarence Blazier, who continued the "Cruises to Nowhere," this time from the city of Santa Monica. The *City of Panama* was licensed to carry a maximum of 453

**The steamer *La Playa* headed out of the Los Angeles harbor bound for nowhere, but filled with booze and gambling tables.**
***Opposite:*** ***La Playa*** **was banned from the Los Angeles harbor, she was sold and her new owner renamed her *City of Panama*.**

passengers on runs not to exceed four hundred miles and within twenty miles of land. Blazier arranged for round-trip customer transportation by water taxi from Santa Monica Pier.

The *City of Panama* operated without interference from any authorities for some weeks. Eventually, however, a group of Santa Monica citizens complained that the role the water taxis were playing in her operation amounted to use of the municipal pier for gambling purposes. The mayor informed them that the city could do nothing, inasmuch as the landing stage of the pier was under long-term franchise to the Olsen Company, which had full control of that area and transportation to and from it. He assured his disapproving constituents, however, that the Santa Monica police chief had sent investigators aboard the *City of Panama*, who reported back that they found no misconduct, nor was there violation of any law occurring within city limits.

The last cruise of the *City of Panama* took place on August 30, 1933. On this night, Robert Moody and Norman Burgess and their respective dates came aboard for a gala evening on the high seas. After the floor show, the four joined other customers who had drifted on deck for a stroll in the fresh sea air. There, the youthful and high-spirited Moody, whom his friends would later describe as a natural-born comedian, began clowning around—doing a comic imitation of the singing and dancing they had just watched on stage.

Fellow passengers gathered round, enjoying his impromptu performance. Others, hearing laughter and applause, left the dining salon and game room to see what was going on and stayed to join the audience. Soon well over a hundred patrons were on the deck, and the roulette wheels and dice tables were losing business.

Crew members warned Moody to "cut it out." He did so, but not quickly enough to prevent ships' bouncers from thrusting him into an area in the lower decks of the vessel's bow that was reserved for unruly visitors. Moody went peaceably, but because he was pushed into the hatch from behind, no one above saw him fall from the narrow ship's ladder, striking his head on the steel deck at the bottom. Three days later, the *Los Angeles Times* reported:

> Federal agents questioned three ship's officers and other members of the Moody party to find out what happened when Robert Moody, a twenty-four-year-old Los Angeles butcher, a passenger on the *City of Panama*, sustained injuries which later resulted in his death.
>
> Inquest will be held September 5 at the coroner's office. No arrests have been made, although "John Doe" warrants have been issued charging murder on the high seas.

At the inquest, the coroner stated young Moody had died of a basal skull fracture "with a history of having been beaten by a member of the *City of Panama*'s crew." The jury heard conflicting versions of what happened after Moody was taken away. His friend Burgess testified:

> I remonstrated when they took him, and I was taken as well. I was beaten about the mouth, handcuffed to a cable near him, saw him beaten mercilessly, and then watched him lying there for three hours, until the ship reached port and we were freed.

Moody's girlfriend, a pretty and well-spoken young woman who much impressed the jury, said that after he was taken away, she did not see him again for three hours, when he was lying prostrate on the deck, moaning and bleeding from the mouth. She reported that she, together with Burgess and his companion, got Moody into the water taxi. Once ashore, they went straight to the Santa Monica police station to file a report, but the sergeant on duty wouldn't take the report and chided them: "Serves him right for going out there in the first place." Thus rebuffed, they took Moody home. When his condition suddenly worsened, he was rushed to the hospital, where he died a few hours later.

*City of Panama* employees at the inquest were Captain John Richardson, First Mate James Ford, and Master-at-Arms (read "Chief Bouncer") John Costello. All three denied Moody had been struck. The first two had not even seen the activity on deck. Costello testified:

I had Burgess halfway down the ladder, when Moody saw us. He ran up the ladder at the same time. Burgess turned to me and in so doing bumped Moody, who fell backward onto the deck.

All three insisted there had been no beatings and that, after his fall, Moody had walked around below decks as if nothing had happened. Furthermore, they concurred, Burgess and Moody were highly intoxicated when they walked off the ship unassisted. No one could explain the coroner's finding that the deceased had a black eye and badly bruised knuckles.

The coroner's jury delivered a verdict of homicide. Federal agents took over the case and requested it go to the grand jury as soon as possible. Costello and Ford were arrested and held on $25,000 bail. At their preliminary hearing, federal Judge Harry Holzer announced he had read the inquest testimony and, because it showed no malice or murderous intent, final charges probably would not exceed manslaughter.

Events had punctured Santa Monica officials' complacent cocoon, and they emerged from it blinking and confused into the glare of unfavorable publicity for their fair city. Mayor Carter pulled himself together, however, and managed to issue a public statement:

> I have arrived at the opinion that the business this ship [*City of Panama*] is engaged in, operating from our municipal pier, is detrimental to the interests of our citizens.

The chief of police was told to investigate the ship's status and turn his report over to the Department of Justice. The city police were to take no active part in the investigation of Moody's death unless and until they were asked to do so by federal agents.

Police Chief Webb found out plenty. The *City of Panama* was still under Panamanian registry. The Panamanian Consul disclosed that this registration was only provisional, not permanent, and that the government of Panama had no intention of extending it while the ship was involved in unsavory activity. Without waiting for any directives from its government, the Consul boarded the vessel and ordered her operators to pay off the crew and close her down immediately and permanently.

Meanwhile, the *Los Angeles Examiner* interviewed the attorney for the ship's real owner, Martin Lewis, who confirmed that Blazier had chartered the *City of Panama* for a full year, but would probably turn her back to Lewis. He implied that would be acceptable, explaining that the ship was to be reconditioned and put into coastal trade, carrying bananas and tomatoes between Mexican, Central American, and Southern California ports. Time would prove that false.

Three and one-half months later, First Mate James Ford and Master-at-Arms John Costello were brought to trial in U.S. District Court, where Federal Judge George Cosgrave determined that the evidence was insufficient and dismissed the case. Nevertheless, the Southland public got the message that gambling ships were run by greedy crooks, carried thugs and gangsters on board, and posed a real danger. Poor Moody's death had accomplished that at least.

But in 1934, Martin Lewis put her under United States registry and changed her name to *Star of*

*Hollywood.* On August 31, 1935, the *Star of Hollywood* dropped anchor just over three miles from Santa Barbara. Reports had it that she had been completely refurbished before coming to Santa Barbara at a cost of $150,000. She was elaborately furnished, sported no fewer than three bars, and contained several private rooms for high rollers. Her trade target may well have been the sizable number of movie moguls and stars who owned magnificent homes in the Montecito area adjacent to Santa Barbara proper.

Santa Barbara officials and a majority of residents hadn't changed their negative attitude about gambling ships ever since the *William H. Harriman*'s unsuccessful attempt to set up shop off the town's beautiful shore. Authorities took immediate steps to prevent the *Star of Hollywood* from operating in local waters. To their surprise, a spokesman for the ship shot back that any such action on their part would lead to a federal injunction suit. Santa Barbara authorities sought advice from Buron Fitts regarding what recourse they had to prevent offshore gambling. They learned that the waters off their shores did not constitute part of a bay as did those off Long Beach, and therefore their best chance was to go after the water taxis instead of the ship itself. Santa Barbara District Attorney Heckendorf continued to envision a raid on the ship.

Undersheriff Jack Ross started a one-man investigation. On opening night, he rode out to the *Star of Hollywood* in one of the several water taxis her proprietors had leased from the H-10 Water Taxi in Long Beach for service at Santa Barbara. His goal was to verify that the "unique entertainment" advertised by the *Star of Hollywood* meant gambling. He returned to shore with eyewitness evidence of her roulette tables, blackjack, craps, and chuck-a-luck games, and a fifty-five-foot-long row of slot machines.

When city and county law enforcers gathered to plot their strategy, they found themselves hopelessly divided over

**The *City of Panama* flies the Panamanian flag in this photograph. When this vessel next appeared as a gambling ship, she was under American registration with the name *Star of Hollywood*.**

the issue of jurisdiction. The *Star of Hollywood* was anchored in what they called "channel waters," between Santa Barbara and the islands of Santa Cruz and Anacapa, two of the Channel Islands chain, which lay about twenty-five miles out to sea. The islands were under Santa Barbara County jurisdiction, so Ross and many others believed that all waters between the shore of Santa Barbara and the shores of the islands were also under county control. Other officials were equally certain that county jurisdiction ended three miles from the city's shore, and then began again three miles landward of the islands. By that reasoning, the floating casino could operate outside county or city jurisdiction anywhere between three miles off Santa Barbara and three miles off the landward side of the islands. After prolonged discussion, it was agreed that state and county jurisdiction ended three miles from the city's shore.

Santa Barbara Police Chief Wilson had little patience with the legal and geographical arguments related to jurisdiction of the ship. He decided he had heard enough theorizing about waters. He went after the taxis by blocking their gangways to prevent passengers from boarding. Within the hour, the chief received a phone call from a Los Angeles attorney, who identified himself as representing the gambling ship's owner. Leaning back in his chair, the chief, whose opinion of "city slicker lawyers" was not the highest, gradually reddened as the caller threatened to start injunction proceedings if he tried to interfere with the ship's activity in any way. The *Star of Hollywood*, the lawyer stated, was outside the three-mile limit and "enjoyed the protection of the United States government." To all that, the chief responded by having his men arrest four H-10 taxi drivers, forcing the operators of the gambling ship to come up with one thousand dollars in bail.

Informed of what was going on, the H-10 Taxi Company now got into the act. It sent its own attorney by plane to San Francisco, where Santa Barbara Superior Court Judge Westwick was visiting. Hearing only one side of the story, the judge obligingly issued a temporary restraining order against interference with the boats operating from Stearns Wharf. The company's owners let Chief Wilson know that once the temporary order became a permanent injunction, they would sue the Santa Barbara Police Department for damages.

Although the chief ceased arresting taxi operators and preventing them from loading passengers, he did continue full surveillance at the wharf. He noticed that the number of passengers was steadily dwindling, and had an idea that the *Star of Hollywood* might soon self-destruct. On the night of September 11, after barely ten days of operation, she went dark. She reopened the next day, but the number of taxis had decreased significantly. On September 14, a notice appeared that the ship would be leaving within the next day or two. Her employees, discharged without pay, began drifting into the city, having come to shore in the sole remaining water taxi. They reported that only three people were still aboard the vessel. The operators had already left, taking with them much of her equipment, the contents of her slot machines, the remaining liquor supply, etc., and had checked out of their Santa Barbara hotel rooms.

On September 16, the arrested taxi drivers appeared in court before Judge Westwick. The city attorney produced so much evidence that they had in fact been violating the state penal code that the judge reversed his previous stand and dissolved the restraining order. The taximen changed their pleas to guilty. Judge Westwick fined each of them $250 or 125 days in jail, of which $245 and 122 days were suspended. Since they had already spent three days in jail, they were thus free to go. The reduction was on condition that both the water taxi and the gambling ship would leave Santa Barbara within twenty-four hours.

As it turned out, the *Star of Hollywood* was already under tow back to the Los Angeles harbor.

She went to San Diego using the name *Reno*, an illegal and unregistered name. But she was closed down after only two months of successful operation and was towed back to Long Beach. She was in trouble with the Customs Department and in violation of the navigation laws. Her owners put her in dry dock, changed her name back to *Star of Hollywood*, and converted her into a barge by removing her propeller.

In 1939, under the ownership of Walter Monstad of Redondo Beach and several co-owners, she became a fishing barge and gambling ship named the *Monte Carlo* (not to be confused with an earlier *Monte Carlo*). After a few months she was towed to Santa Monica, where her name was changed yet again to *Texas*. She anchored a short distance from the *Rex*.

## The *Texas*

When Earl Warren launched his simultaneous raids on the gambling ships off the coast of Southern California on August 1, 1939, the *Texas* was among them. Ignoring the protests of Captain Walter Monstad, Jahnsen and his deputies forced their way onto the *Texas*, handcuffing Monstad for good measure. Next, Jahnsen ordered Monstad to have the ship towed to San Pedro, threatening to wreck all her equipment if he refused. When Monstad refused, the wrecking began in full view of customers still aboard. Deputies smashed furniture, roulette wheels, and craps tables and tossed the parts into the sea. Even slot machines—their coin contents removed—went over the rail. Not until a Coast Guard cutter patrolling the area came abreast of the gambling ship, did the veritable orgy of destruction cease. As night settled in, the situation aboard the *Texas* had reached an impasse. Jahnsen had carried out his threat. Monstad and other co-owners who were aboard continued to refuse to have the vessel towed, much less to agree to surrender her. Suddenly, someone pulled the main switch of the ship's electrical system and plunged her into total darkness. Naturally, no member of the ship's personnel would tell the confused deputies where the switch was located and, unfortunately for Jahnsen, his preliminary undercover investigators had failed to include that detail in their reports. The whole atmosphere was turning ugly when, as suddenly as they had gone out, the lights came on again.

At that point, Monstad reluctantly agreed to Jahnsen's demand that the *Texas* close down and not attempt to reopen there or elsewhere.

The attorneys for the *Texas* announced they were filing a million-dollar civil suit against all officials

**Opposite:** Authorities set up a booking system on the *Texas* and Wilbert Monstad, one of her owners, is fingerprinted here (top left). The raiders on the *Texas* wrecked gambling equipment and furniture, and threw it into the ocean. The Coast Guard ordered them to cease because the detritus was a menace to navigation.

Cruises to Nowhere

NOIR AFLOAT

responsible for wrecking the gambling equipment. Tugs towed her to San Pedro, where she remained tied to a dock for more than a year. She was never used as a gambling ship again.

In 1940, Captain Charles Arnold leased her from owner Walter Monstad and brought her back to Santa Monica. Arnold, a longtime resident of Santa Monica, had owned and operated the popular fishing barge *Star of Scotland* ex-*Kenilworth*, until Tony Cornero purchased her from him and transformed her into the mighty *Rex*. When Arnold was operating that ship as a fishing barge, the City of Santa Monica had given him a ten-year lease of space on its municipal pier. When he later allowed the space to be used as a launching pad for water taxi service to the *Rex*, frustrated and furious city officials found themselves surprisingly hamstrung in their frantic efforts to deprive him of the lease.

Perhaps out of fond memory of his previous ship, Arnold renamed the *Texas* the *Star of Scotland*. He tried operating her as a floating nightclub, but without any gambling, patrons were few and far between. Giving up on that enterprise, Arnold turned her back into a fishing barge. America's entry into World War II in December 1941, however, brought about stricter limitations on civilian ships anchored at sea. These, plus the fact that seawater was entering the barge faster than her bilge pumps could handle it, caused him to give up his lease on the vessel and return her to Monstad. At that time there was no dry dock available for a civilian ship, so he had

*Opposite:* Contreras checked out the gambling equipment on the *Texas* prior to it being sent ashore (top left). Crowds of curious spectators line up on Santa Monica Pier to watch *Orca* unload its unusual cargo (bottom). The tug was filled with gambling equipment from the *Texas*, which was now ready to head for shore (top right).
*Above:* The *Texas* was leased again and transformed into a fishing barge that was named in honor of the *Star of Scotland*.

to wait. Because of that, the *Star of Scotland* ex-*Texas* remained anchored off Santa Monica, out of use and staffed only by watchmen.

On the night of January 23, 1942, three frightened on-duty watchmen fired a distress flare from the deck of the former gambling ship. The glare in the sky alerted Santa Monica lifeguards, who sped out to her in a rescue boat. The watchmen, working frantically, called out that they were afraid they could not keep the ship afloat much longer. The men had contacted Monstad by radiophone, and he and Captain Harry Wilson arrived shortly thereafter with extra pumps and went aboard. All five men fought desperately to save the vessel by patching and sealing her rusty and splitting seams. After about five or six hours at a hopeless task, calamity brought the truth home. A huge swell hit the side of the ship with such force that it opened even more seams, and the sea rushed in to claim her. By 4:30 in the morning, the *Star of Scotland* ex-*Texas*, ex-*Star of Hollywood*, ex-*City of Panama*, ex-*La Playa*, ex-*La Playa Ensenada*, ex-*Chiapas*, ex-H.M.S. *Mistletoe*, filled with water and sank to the bottom of the ocean.

Lifeboats capsized, and watchman William Gillette was drowned. While one of the Santa Monica lifeguards leaped into the water to retrieve his body, the others successfully rescued the remaining four men from the waves.

No end of confusion resulted from this mishap. Because of wartime censorship, newspapers could not print detailed articles about the sinking of a ship. The puzzlement came because of the name *Star of Scotland*. There were two different ships sailing at the same time with the name *Star of Scotland*. First there was the original *Star of Scotland* ex-*Kenilworth* that became the gambling ship *Rex*. After her gambling career, she changed to a six-masted schooner and was given back her original name *Star of Scotland*. Second, after Charles Arnold leased the ex-gambling ship *Texas*, he converted her to a fishing barge. He sentimentally named her after his original fishing barge, the four-masted bark *Star of Scotland* that became the gambling ship *Rex*. One of the two ships with the name *Star of Scotland* sank, but it wasn't clear which one.

The gambling ship *Texas* rests on the ocean floor off Santa Monica under seventy feet of water, and still attracts visitors. She serves as a popular treasure-hunt site for scuba divers and a home for fish and other sea life who have no need to roll the dice or make a bet on a full house.

In January of 1942, the old vessel with the name *Star of Scotland* (ex-*Texas*, ex-*Star of Hollywood*, ex-*Reno*, ex-*City of Panama*, ex-*La Playa*, ex-*La Playa Ensenada*, ex-*Chiapas*, ex-H.M.S. *Mistletoe*) filled with water and sank deep into Santa Monica Bay. Owner Walter Monstad and two Santa Monica harbormasters viewed the top of her mast after the ship sank.

# Bibliography

Anderson, Clinton H. *Beverly Hills is My Beat*. Englewood Cliffs, New Jersey: Prentice-Hall, 1960.

Andrews, Ralph W. *Redwood Classic*. New York: Bonanza Books, 1958.

Arnold, Craig. "Donald Warren: *Star of Scotland* Survivor." Maritime Museum Association of San Diego, *Mains'l Haul* XXV (Fall 1988).

Barber, Lawrence. *Tango Around the Horn: The World War II Voyage of America's Last Large Sailing Ship*. Portland: Oregon Maritime Center and Museum, 1991.

Beigel, Harvey M. *Battleship Country: The Battle Fleet at San Pedro-Long Beach, California, 1919-1940*. Missoula, Montana: Pictorial Histories Publishing, 1983.

"Bets Becalmed." *Newsweek*, August 19, 1946.

Brown, Giles T. *Ships that Sail No More; Marine Transportation from San Diego to Puget Sound, 1910-1940*. Lexington: University of Kentucky Press, 1966.

"California Police Go Outside Three-Mile Limit to Fight 'Battle of Santa Monica Bay'" *Life Magazine*, August 14, 1939. Pp. 18-19.

California Commission on Organized Crime. *The Special Crime Study Commission on Organized Crime*. State of California, Sacramento, California, May 11, 1953.

Cardone, Bonnie J., and Patrick Smith. *Shipwrecks of Southern California*. Birmingham, Alabama: Menasha Ridge Press, 1989.

Colton, J. Ferrell. "A Marine Metamorphosis—Four-Masted Bark to Six-Masted Schooner." *Trident Magazine*.

Creel, George. "Unholy City." *Collier's*, September 2, 1939.

"Crime, Chance on the High Seas." *Time Magazine*, August 14, 1939.

Demaris, Ovid. *The Last Mafioso: The Treacherous World of Jimmy Fratianno*. New York: Times Books, 1981.

*Dictionary of American Naval Fighting Ships*. Vol. V & VI. Washington, D.C.: Navy Department, 1959.

Duncan, Fred B. *Deepwater Family*. New York: Pantheon Books, 1969.

Eppinga, Jane. "Windjammer Finale." *Prologue Quarterly of the National Archives* Vol. 25, no. 3 (Fall 1993).

"Everybody Gambles: First Pictures on Gaming Ship *Tango*." *Life Magazine*, January 10, 1938. Pp. 47-48.

Fey, Marshall. *Slot Machines: A Pictorial History of the First 100 Years of the World's Most Popular Coin-Operated Gaming Device*. Reno, Nevada: Liberty Bell Books, 1989.

Finney, Guy Woodward. *Angel City in Turmoil*. Los Angeles: Amer Press, 1945.

_____. *The Great Los Angeles Bubble*. Los Angeles: Milton Forbes Company, 1929.

"Gambling Ship." *Life Magazine*, August 19, 1946. Pp. 34-35.

Geddes, Robert N. *Slot Machines on Parade*. Long Beach, California: Mead Company, 1980.

Gibbs, Jim. *Pacific Square-Riggers: Pictorial History of the Great Windships of Yesteryear*. New York: Bonanza Books, 1977.

Giesler, Jerry, and Pete Martin. *The Jerry Giesler Story*. New York: Simon and Schuster, 1960.

Grover, David H. *U.S. Army Ships and Watercraft of World War II*. Annapolis, Maryland: Naval Institute Press, 1987.

Harmon, Wendell E. "The Bootlegger Era in Southern California." Historical Society of Southern California, *The Quarterly* (December 1955).

Heimann, Jim. *Out with the Stars: Hollywood Nightlife in the Golden Era*. New York: Abbeville Press, 1985.

Hennessy, Mark William. *The Sewall Ships of Steel*. Augusta, Maine: Kennebec Journal Press, 1937.

Henstell, Bruce. "Now Those Really Were 'Floating' Crap Games." *Los Angeles Magazine*, December 1978.

_____. *Sunshine and Wealth: Los Angeles in the Twenties and Thirties*. San Francisco: Chronicle Books, 1984.

Hurst, Alexander Anthony. *The Medley of Mast and Sail II: A Camera Record*. Annapolis, Maryland: Naval Institute Press, 1981.

Huycke, Harold D. *To Santa Rosalia Further and Back*. Newport News, Virginia: Mariners Museum, 1970.

Jennings, Dean Southern. *We Only Kill Each Other: The Life and Bad Times of Bugsy Siegel*. Englewood Cliffs, New Jersey: Prentice-Hall, 1967.

Katcher, Leo. *Earl Warren: A Political Biography*. New York: McGraw-Hill, 1967.

Kaufman, Perry. *The Best City of Them All: A History of Las Vegas, 1930-1960*. Diss., University of California, Santa Barbara, 1974.

Kemble, John Haskell. *San Francisco Bay: A Pictorial Maritime History*. Cambridge, Maryland: Cornell Maritime Press, 1957.

Kooiman, William. "*Star of Scotland*'s Many Lives." *Sea Classics*, May 1991. pp. 40-45.

"Lady Luck Goes to Sea." *Loose Change* Magazine, Vol. 5 No. 1 & 2, January/February 1983.

"The Last Six-Masted Schooner, *Cidade do Porto*." *Tiller Magazine*, April 1947.

*Lloyds Register of Shipping 1891-1953*. London, England: Committee of Lloyds.

Lubbock, Basil. *The Down Easters: American Deep-Water Sailing Ships 1869-1929*. Glasgow: Brown, Son & Ferguson, 1980.

Lyman, John. *Pacific Owned Sailers That Were Built Elsewhere from 1900-1941*. Marine Digest, 1941.

Mandel, Leo. *William Fiske Harrah: The Life and Times of a Gambling Magnate*. Garden City, New York: Doubleday, 1982.

"A Marine Metamorphosis—From Bark to Schooner." *Trident Magazine*.

Marshall, Don B. *California Shipwrecks: Footsteps in the Sea*. Seattle, Washington: Superior Publishing Company, 1978.

Matthews, Frederick C. *American Merchant Ships, 1850-1900*. New York: Dover Publications, 1987.

McKinney, Dwight F., and Fred Allhoff. "The Lid Off Los Angeles." *Liberty Magazine*, November 11, 18, 25, December 2, 9, 16, 1939.

*The Mercantile Navy List and Maritime Directory for 1922*. London: Majesty's Stationery Office, 1922.

Messick, Hank, and Burt Goldblatt. *The Only Game in Town: An Illustrated History of Gambling*. New York: Crowell, 1976.

"Misunderstood Man." *Time Magazine*, August 19, 1946.

Moehring, Eugene P. *Resort City in the Sunbelt: Las Vegas, 1930-1970*. Reno: University of Nevada Press, 1989.

Muir, Florabel. "Gambling Ship." *The Saturday Evening Post*, August 12, 1939.

Muir, Florabel. *Headline Happy*. New York: Holt, 1950.

Newell, Gordon R. *SOS North Pacific: Tales of Shipwrecks off the Washington, British Columbia and Alaska Coasts*. Portland, Oregon: Binfords & Mort, 1955.

_____. *The H.W. McCurdy Marine History of the Pacific Northwest, 1895-1965*. Seattle: Superior Publishing Company, 1966.

Newell, Gordon R., and Joe Williamson. *Pacific Lumber Ships*. Seattle: Superior Publishing Company, 1960.

Newmark, Marco R. "Ordinances and Regulations of Los Angeles, Part II." Historical Society of Southern California, *The Quarterly* (June 1948).

*The Northern Barrage, Mine Force, United States Atlantic Fleet, the North Sea, 1918*. Annapolis, Maryland: U.S. Naval Institute, 1919.

Parish, James Robert., and Steven Whitney. *The George Raft File: The Unauthorized Biography*. New York: Drake, 1973.

Pollack, Jack Harrison. *Earl Warren, the Judge Who Changed America*. Englewood Cliffs, New Jersey: Prentice-Hall, 1979.

**Bibliography**

Rappleye, Charles, and Ed Becker. *All-American Mafioso: The Johnny Rosselli Story*. New York: Doubleday, 1991.

*Record of American and Foreign Shipping 1912*. New York: American Bureau of Shipping.

Reid, Ed, and Ovid Demaris. *The Green Felt Jungle*. New York: Trident Press, 1963.

Richardson, James Hugh. *For the Life of Me: Memoirs of a City Editor*. New York: Putnam, 1954.

Robinson, W.W. *Lawyers of Los Angeles: A History of the Los Angeles Bar Association and of the Bar of Los Angeles County*. Los Angeles: Los Angeles Bar Association, 1959.

Roeburt, John. *Get Me Giesler*. New York: Belmont Books, 1962.

Rohwer, Jurgen. *Axis Submarine Success 1939-1945*. Annapolis, Maryland: Naval Institute Press, 1983.

Scarne, John. *Complete Guide to Gambling*. New York: Simon and Schuster, 1961.

Scheina, Robert L. *U.S. Coast Guard Cutters and Craft, 1946-1990*. Annapolis, Maryland: Naval Institute Press, 1990.

Seymour, Dale. *Antique Gambling Chips: With Price Guide & Chip Codes*. Palo Alto, California: Past Pleasures, 1985.

"The *Star of Scotland*, A Varied Career as a Four-Masted Bark and Six-Masted Schooner." *North American Cape Horners, Edmonds, Washington: a Newsletter for Members and Associates* Vol. 1, No. 3 (June 1994).

Turner, Wallace. *Gamblers' Money, the New Force in American Life*. Boston: Houghton Mifflin, 1965.

Tygiel, Jules. *The Great Los Angeles Swindle: Oil, Stocks, and Scandal during the Roaring Twenties*. New York: Oxford University Press, 1994.

U.S. Department of Commerce. *American Documented Seagoing Merchant Vessels of 500 Gross Tons and Over*. Washington, D.C.: Government Printing Office, 1923.

U.S. Department of Commerce. *Merchant Vessels of the United States*. Washington, D.C.: Government Printing Office, 1884-1931.

U.S. Department of the Navy. Naval History Division. *America's Naval Fighting Ships*. Washington, D.C.: Government Printing Office, 1976.

Vale, Rena M. "A New Boss Takes Los Angeles." *The American Mercury*, March 1941.

Viehe, Fred W. "The Recall of Mayor Frank L. Shaw: A Revision." The Magazine of the California Historical Society, *California History* (Winter 1980/81).

Warren, Earl. *The Memoirs of Earl Warren*. Garden City, N.Y.: Doubleday, 1977.

White, Leslie T. *Me, Detective*. New York: Harcourt, Brace and Company, 1936.

Willoughby, Malcolm Francis. *Rum War at Sea*. Washington, D.C.: Government Printing Office, 1964.

Witter, Jere. "The Wild Reign of Captain Tony and His Floating Casinos." *Los Angeles Magazine*, March 1965.

Wykes, Alan. *The Complete Illustrated Guide to Gambling*. Garden City, New York: Doubleday, 1964.

Yablonsky, Lewis. *George Raft*. New York: McGraw-Hill, 1974.


**Other Resources**


Darnell, Earl, dealer on *Rex*. Interview by author.

MacLean, Don, able-bodied seaman on *Tango*, 1937 to 1939. Interview by author.

Telande, Robert, shore boat operator for *Rex* and *Star of Hollywood*. Interview by author.

California State Archives. Earl Warren Papers. DR2725-2726 F 3640: 2624-2636 1943-1953.

Federal Bureau of Investigation. Files of Tony Cornero Stralla and Fred Grange: 65-4975, 64-27107, 5-4031.

National Archives, Washington D.C., Record Group: 041 Marine and Inspection and Navigation (ship documentation):

- *Bunker Hill*, Official No. 204264 R6/27/5
- *James Tuft*, Official No. 77454 R3/9/4
- *Johanna Smith*, Official No. 215021 R6/23/5
- *Monfalcone*, Official No. 219468 R7/1/4
- *Monte Carlo*, ex-*McKittrick*, Official No. 223209 R7/9/4
- *Mount Baker*, Official No. 216217 R6/34/3
- *Rex*, ex-*Star of Scotland*, ex-*Kenilworth*, Official No. 14494 R3/4/3
- *Star of Hollywood*, Official No. 232927 R7/9/4
- *Tango*, ex-*Mary Dollar*, ex-*Hans*, Official No. 221994 R7/4/4
- *William H. Harriman*, Official No. 219398 R7/1/3


Statutes of California, Second Session of the Legislature, 1851.

Statutes of California, Regular Session of the 48th Legislature, 1929.

California State Assembly. AB 3769, An Act to add 11319 to the Penal Code, relating to gaming. Introduced by Mickey Conroy (R-Santa Ana) 1993.

Minutes of the Santa Monica Board of Trustees and the Santa Monica City Council on the Beach, January 3, 1887 to August 27, 1941.

Minutes of the Santa Monica Board of Trustees and Santa Monica City Council on Piers and Wharfs, February 13, 1888 to February 21, 1940.

United States House of Representatives. Hearings before the Subcommittee on Navigation Laws of the Committee on Merchant Marine, Radio, and Fisheries. 72nd Congress First Session on H.R. 408 and S.2883, March 29, 1932.

United States Senate. Special Committee to Investigate Organized Crime in Interstate Commerce, 81st and 82nd Congress 1951. Parts 2, 5, 10.


Noel Pemberton Billing v. J. Dale Gentry, Harry Wilson, and H.G. McKinney (1930) United States District Court, No. 4291-C. RG 21, Records of the United States District Court for the Southern District of California, National Archives-Pacific Southwest Region, Laguna Niguel, California.

Jack Cavallero v. S.S. *Tango*, et al., No. 3282-Y.

*Ex parte* Chase et al., 119 Cal. App. 432, 6 P. 2nd 577 (1931).

E.C. Genereaux, et al. v. S.S. *Star of Hollywood*, et al., No. 6756-M.

Mrs. Aron Kirby v. Captain Charles Arnold and Lew Lockhart, No. 8292-H.

New Jersey v. City of New York, 283 U.S. 473, 75L.Ed. 1176, 51 S.Ct. 519.

People v. Chase et al., 1 P. 2d 60 (1931).

People v. Shaw, et al., Cr.4339, 112 P.2d 241 (1941).

People v. Stralla, et al., 14 Cal.2d 617 (1939).

People v. Stralla, et al., 88 P.2d 736, (1939).

People v. Stralla, Opinion No. 443, 429.

Rex, Inc. v. Superior Court in and for Los Angeles County, 34 Cal. App.2nd 96 (1939).

Soule v. S.S. *Tango*, Inc., a Corp., No. 8127-RJ.

United States v. The Barge *Bunker Hill*, Her Tackle, Apparel, Furniture, Equipment and Cargo, No. 5766-O'C.

United States v. California, 381 U.S. 139, 174 (1965).

United States v. Carrillo *et al.*, 13 F. Supp. 121 (1935).

United States v. Carl Carrillo *et al.*, No. 12517-S. RG 21, Records of the United States District Court for the Southern District of California, National Archives-Pacific Southwest Region, Laguna Niguel, California.

United States v. Frank Cornero, No. 6293. RG 21, Records of the United States District Court for the Southern District of California, National Archives-Pacific Southwest Region, Laguna Niguel, California.

United States v. Tony Cornero, No. 6617-Crim. RG 21, Records of the United States District Court for the Southern District of California, National Archives-Pacific Southwest Region, Laguna Niguel, California.

United States v. Tony Cornero, No. 9579-M. RG 21, Records of the United States District Court for the Southern District of California, National Archives-Pacific Southwest Region, Laguna Niguel, California.

United States v. The Steamship *Johanna Smith* (1928), Civil Law File 3257.

United States v. Motor Schooner *Przemysl*, Her Engine, Equipment, and Tackle.

United States v. Marvin E. Schouweiler, No. 8710-J.

United States v. Ed V. Turner, No. 12157-J. RG 21, Records of the United States District Court for the Southern District of California, National Archives-Pacific Southwest Region, Laguna Niguel, California.


*Las Vegas Review-Journal*.

*Long Beach Press-Telegram*.

*Long Beach Sun*.

*Los Angeles Examiner*.

*Los Angeles Times*.

*Morning Press* (Santa Barbara, California).

*New York Times*.

*Orange Daily News*.

*Oregonian* (Portland).

*Newport-Balboa Times*.

*San Diego Union*.

*San Francisco Chronicle*.

*Santa Monica Evening Outlook*.

*Ventura Free Press*.

# Photograph Credits

The author expresses sincere appreciation to the individuals and institutions that generously contributed photographs for this book. Should there be an omission, the author apologizes, and upon notification, a correction will be made in future editions.

All dice, chips and ephemera related to the gambling ships are from the author's collection, as are the following photographs: 9, 10, 11, 13 (Dragna), 14 (Porter), 26-32, 40, 41, 42 (bottom right), 44, 45, 61, 66, 71, 99, 101, 102, 115, 124, 126-129, 145-147, 169, 181 (bottom), 183-186, 188, 199.

Bill Beebe: 12 (Contreras), 49, 52, 53, 81, 85, 87, 89-91, 95 (upper and lower left), 96, 198, 201.

California State Library: 12 (Warren).

Bruce Henstell: 8, 14 (Shaw), 19, 51, 58, 73, 79, 94, 95 (upper right), 103, 115, 117, 166.

Historical Society of Long Beach: 36, 37, 118-119, 170-174, 176, 177.

Los Angeles Public Library: 12 (Biscailuz), 17, 39, 132.

San Diego Historical Society—Ticor Collection: 180, 181 (top).

San Francisco Maritime National Park: 35, 120, 158, 164, 168, 175.

San Francisco Public Library: 130.

Sherman Library and Gardens: 34, 42 (upper left), 43, 144, 160-162, 190.

UCLA Special Collections: 108.

USC Regional History Collection: 12 (Fitts), 13 (Keyes, McAfee, Marco), 14 (Bowron, Cryer), 15, 16, 57, 59, 75, 97, 104, 105, 107, 109, 111, 123, 136-140, 143, 178, 187, 194, 197.

# Acknowledgments

Through the years many people touched this undertaking and left their most welcome mark. First and foremost, I owe an enormous debt of gratitude to Robert Schwemmer for the ship and maritime history. His relentless research from his personal library and the holdings of the federal archives proved to be invaluable.

Maritime historian Captain Harold D. Huycke read the original text of this book. His most welcome contributions assured credibility to the information and prevented me from making inexcusable blunders.

Thomas Curry showed me how to organize the abundance of reference material collected for this book. Bettye Ellison and the late Tom Owen at the Los Angeles Public Library revealed their interest in this project, extending a generous amount of time and effort in finding materials. Dace Taube of the University of Southern California History Center contributed extraordinary service. She made researching a pleasure with her friendly, helpful attitude. William O. Hendricks at the Sherman Library in Costa Mesa made that library's wonderful maritime photograph collection available to me. Zona Gale Forbes at the Historical Society of Long Beach made a relentless search for gambling ship photographs in their collection. Suzanne Dewberry of the National Archives in Laguna Niguel contributed her fabulous expertise in finding records in that mammoth repository.

Then to get off the beaten path I turned to casino chip and token collectors to see if they could lead me to where I might find dice, chips, and other items created by the gambling ships. Stephen Alpert, Jack Boberg, J. Scott Fawcett, Ernie Wheelden, and Ron and Norma Hazelton, with their vast knowledge of gambling casino paraphernalia, helped me find some of the uncommon pieces used as illustrations in this book. Sonja Jensen and Fred Grange, Jr., made available FBI files, acquired through the Freedom of Information Act, about Tony Cornero Stralla and their father, Fred Grange. I sincerely thank Bill Beebe for allowing the use of the extraordinary photographs of the raid on the *Rex* taken by the late Emerson Gale.

Closer to home, family members expressed an interest in this project and contributed their expertise. My daughter Monica Marquez, an attorney, showed me how to find my way through the maze of legal files and court records. My daughter Eileen Bonaduce patiently guided me through the early stages of learning how to use a computer, and my son Ernesto read the manuscript and contributed his suggestions. My wife Lois took my rough manuscript in hand and rewrote it. She transformed it into readable text, for which I am most grateful.

Two dear friends, Warren and Dorothy Thompson, read the manuscript and offered their most welcome critique.

Amy Inouye of Future Studio brought her terrific design talent to the layout of the book you are now reading. Thanks also to Stephanie Palermini of Angel City Press for her astute observations and comments.

My special thanks to Angel City Press publishers Paddy Calistro and Scott McAuley for believing in me and the importance of this book.

### S.S. TANGO
## The World's Largest Pleasure Ship
UNDER MANAGEMENT OF CLARENCE BLAZIER

The Management of the
## SHOW BOAT MONTE CARLO
cordially extends to you, and your party, an invitation to be their guest at dinner, on the high seas, aboard the Largest Pleasure Ship in the World, at any time convenient to yourself.     (ADULTS ONLY)

DINNER SERVED UNTIL MIDNITE

SPEED BOATS LEAVE DAILY FROM
## 1275 West 7th Street
LONG BEACH (First Parking Lot)
EVERY FIFTEEN MINUTES STARTING AT 6 P. M. — SATURDAYS
SUNDAYS AND HOLIDAYS AT 1 P. M.
TELEPHONES: Long Beach 625-93 and 608-17

DINE · DANCE · RELAX

*The Management of the*
## SHOW BOAT MONTE CARLO
*cordially extends to you, and your party, adults only, an invitation to be their guest at dinner, on the high seas, aboard the largest Amusement Ship in the World.*
*Dinner served until 11:30 p.m.*

Speed Boats leave every 15 minutes from the City Water Taxi Company's new location, 7th and Pico, Long Beach, Calif., (First Parking Lot), Starting at 6:00 P.M. daily — 1:00 P.M. Saturdays, Sundays and Holidays.
Telephones: Long Beach 625-93 and 608-17

### THE GREAT WHITEWAY TO JOYLAND

## s.s. REX
OFF SANTA MONICA PIER
ANCHORED IN CALM WATERS
BEYOND THE 3 MILE LIMIT
LION MATCH CO. INC. LOS ANGELES 13, CAL.
CLOSE COVER BEFORE STRIKING

## S.S. TANGO
ANCHORED OFF LONG BEACH, CALIF.
*The World's Largest Pleasure Ship*
CROWN MATCH CO. LOS ANGELES

The Panama liner La Playa is a modern all-steel, ocean liner of 1450 tons gross registry. 2500 h.p. engines. Cruising speed 11 knots per hr. Full electric system, with auxiliary unit. Complete all-steel life boat equipment, holding entire passenger list and crew. Has experienced licensed Captain and officers, with full crew.

Board the ship itself at the Dock, Berth 60 Outer Harbor, San Pedro.

## SAILING EVERY NIGHT 7:30
Returning 1:30 A.M.
Extra Cruise
Sunday Afternoon 1 P.M.
Returning 6:30 P.M.

The S.S. La Playa was constructed by the eminent Scotch shipbuilders, Greenocks and Grangemouth Dockyards Co., Ltd., Grangemouth, Scotland. Certified by United States Steamboat Inspection Service. Surveyed and Registered by Lloyd's of London. Operated under the Laws of the Republic of Panama.

Passage Round Trip $2

BERTH 60

## S.S. TANGO
OFF OCEAN PARK AMUSEMENT PIER
OPEN 24 HOURS DAILY!
### UNLIMITED ACTION!

Racing Results From All Tracks Daily 9 a.m.
## WE PAY TRACK ODDS!
*No Insurance*
Caliente Racing Description Every Sunday

5th Year Under Same Management
FASTEST SPEEDBOATS LEAVE EVERY 10 MINUTES
Only 12 Min. to S. S. Tango
ROUND TRIP 25c

Follow the Big RED "T" to Ocean Park

OCEAN PARK AMUSEMENT PIER
1000 CAR CONCRETE PARKING LOT

S.S.TANGO

ALL STEEL! FIREPROOF!

DINING DANCING Entertainment 2 BARS

### Largest and Finest Pleasure Ship on the Pacific

LION MATCH CO. NEW YORK
S.S. MONTE CARLO
DINING & DANCING
NO COUVERT CHARGE
PHONES 62593 679-287

S.S. MONTE CARLO
Boats leave every 15 minutes from 1375 W. 7th St. LONG BEACH
CLOSE COVER BEFORE STRIKING

SIX GOLDEN HOURS ON THE HIGH SEAS
DINING—DANCING TEMPTING REFRESHMENTS SPORTIVE ADVENTURE

SAILING 7:30 EVERY NITE
RETURNING 1:30 A.M.
Extra Cruise Sunday 1 p.m. Return 6:30 p.m.

DINNER DE L $1.50
No Cover Charge
PASSAGE $2 Round Trip

Tickets on sale without extra charge at
GITTELSON BROS. TICKET OFFICES
6615 Hollywood Blvd — HOlly 3131 Lankershim Hotel Biltmore Hotel
Or Any Theatre Ticket Broker Mitchell Branch Ticket Offices
Also at Dock, Berth 60, San Pedro Outer Harbor

## S.S. La PLAYA

## S.S. CALIENTE
*The Pleasure Palace of the Pacific*

SPEEDBOATS FOR HIRE
are available at
## 1315 West Seventh Street
(One Block West of Pico Ave.)
### LONG BEACH
LOOK FOR THE RED SIGN "TANGO"
Fare 25c Round Trip - - - Free Parking

TURF INFORMATION
Complete Race Results from 9:30 A.M. until ?

GUEST CARD
THE STAR OF HOLLYWOOD

(The Pacific Coast's Finest Pleasure Ship)
CORDIALLY INVITES you and your party (adults) to be guests for an evening of Dining, Dancing, and thrilling Fun aboard the Ship, anchored just 15 minutes off Newport Beach
Water Taxis leave from Newport Pier every 15 minutes from 9:30 A.M. until the wee hours—Sundays 1 P.M.
ROUND TRIP TAXI FARE 25c
Complete Cafe Service and Cocktail Bar Aboard Serving at Shore Prices

(OVER)     Present this card at Dining Room for Complimentary Din...